UNTIL HOPE RETURNS

First Printing: 2018

ISBN-13: 978-0-9990716-3-2 (Paperback edition)
ISBN-13: 978-0-9990716-4-9 (Hardcover edition)
ISBN-13: 978-0-9990716-5-6 (eBook edition)

LCCN: 2018941269

For more information about this or other Grassleaf works, please visit grassleafpublishing.com or email info@grassleafpublishing.com.

I created Grassleaf Publishing because I believe good literary works, films, music, and art of all types can come from anywhere and anyone. After all, all goodness comes from He who created goodness, and He is powerful enough to display that goodness through any individual.

As my writing turned from a personal hobby into a passion, I quickly learned that I had no chance to see my work be published without a platform with thousands of followers. This was disappointing as a writer, but also disheartening as a reader. What kind of good works am I missing out on?

So, a new calling developed for me, and instead of trying to coax agents and publishers into publishing my books, I decided to start my own publishing company.

Publishers will tell us that people do not read anymore. They blame the old-fashioned, boring art of reading. However, when one inspects the quality of books being printed, it is easy to see why consumers have turned away. Books are published based on the name of the author, not the quality of the content. Occasionally, a good book will make its way through, and readers will devour it over a weekend…especially young readers. So, it isn't the art of reading that's old-fashioned.

At Grassleaf Publishing, it is believed that good books can still be written. But the process of publishing must evolve. That's why Grassleaf operates differently than the traditional publishing company. Content and quality are the sole focus. The status, background, or life experience of an author doesn't matter. Grassleaf Publishing believes that if good content is made available, He will see that it serves its purpose.

As a reader, you may not recognize Grassleaf's authors, but hopefully you will recognize our logo and trust that it represents a worthwhile work.

Grassleaf Publishing was created to do one thing: contribute a verse.

– Charles Brandon Wagoner

Praise for
Until Hope Returns

"Tom Norvell has created a pitch perfect collection of stories, insights, and biblically based teachings that reflect years of observation on the human condition and the ways of God. Each is short enough for a quick read, and long enough for a consistent take-away. You will find Tom a great companion day after day."
– Andrew Reese, PE LEED, Vice President, AMEC Foster
  Wheeler Americas – Environment & Infrastructure
  Author of *Bleats 365* (2015) and Co-Author of *Freedom Tools: For
  Overcoming Life's Tough Problems* (2015)

"*Until Hope Returns* is a work born of faith, love, and hope. The devotional thoughts contained in these chapters reflect years of walking in the footsteps of our Savior and wrestling with real life issues. You will find authenticity, reality, and genuine brokenness within these pages. You will also find yourself and your spiritual journey woven within the tapestry of this very transparent and relevant work by Tom.

"I highly recommend *Until Hope Returns*. It will challenge you, stretch you, comfort you…and always leave you with a deep sense of hope…for the remainder of your own journey in this life."
– Rick Fancher, Business Development Specialist, PAX EQUITY

"Tom Norvell writes with the heart of a pastor and the mind of a father. In his writing presence you feel safe and hopeful. Read this book and trust that God is as good as Tom suggests."
– Josh Graves, Teaching Minister, Otter Creek Church of Christ

"My friend, Tom, is a wordsmith, much more than a good writer. And his latest collection of words has been carefully shaped by him into a wonderful spiritual travel guide. The pages lead us on a quest – a mutual quest beyond tradition and orthodoxy. Read with a pen in hand; you will write your own book as you read.

"Each chapter takes us to a reflective vista, a musing spot. His warm and penetrating questions force us to look again, to unlearn, and rethink. Together, we begin with something familiar and end up unpacking the unexpected. So, take your time…enjoy the journey. Along the way you will get to know my friend, Tom…and another side of yourself."
– Ron Rose, Founder, President, Faith Coaching Network

"If you need encouragement, read this book. If you are an encourager, read this book. Life can be simpler. God is closer. Tom Norvell has a way with words. He is an encourager. He is a coach. He knows hardship and he knows joy. He takes "everyday occurrences" and helps us see God at work."

(Might add ... I would still be referring my patients to him for encouragement and counseling if he had not moved away.)

– Dr. Glenn Beasley

"*Until Hope Returns* brings together a collection of insights, brief and pointed, as sensitive culturally as they are rich spiritually. Tom Norvell, pastor and counselor, speaker and writer, teacher and friend, draws on a lifetime of ministry, of service to the hurting, of experience as a gentle and attentive friend to those who face life's deepest, most troubling dilemmas.

"Tom shares out of his abundant time in prayer and study, from countless hours as a listening companion, and from his own personal encounter with tragedy and disappointment. He emerges as a faithful and wise resource for those of us who would follow Jesus. His special gift as author and pastor is a ready grasp of the culture, the ability to understand intuitively the intersections of contemporary life with the mind and spirit of the Christian believer. To read *Until Hope Returns* is to enjoy intimate conversation with one who discerns the loving and majestic hand of God in the small matters of life, and who knows how to encourage people of faith on our journey with Jesus. It is to enjoy a much-needed coffee break with a thoughtful and reliable confidante. I'll turn to this book often in the best of times and the worst of times."

– Mark Tucker, former Dean of Library & Information Resources at Abilene Christian University and Professor Emeritus, Purdue University

UNTIL HOPE RETURNS

Tom Norvell

Dedication

The book you hold in your hands or are reading on your electronic device has been a labor, a joy, a challenge, a dream come true, and often times my therapy. I dedicate it to the three people who mean more to me than life itself.

Grant and Laura, so much of what I've written is a result of being your dad. When you were born and placed in my arms a whole new way of understanding God and how He feels about His children was revealed to me. I have been grateful to have played a part in guiding you through some of the toughest challenges you have faced. I have been privileged to pray for you when I could do nothing else as I was forced to sit back and watch as you learned to make your own way. I have marveled as God revealed His plan to bring Bethany and Alex into our family. As I watch you flourish in your own marriages and display so much love and gentleness to Isabel, Hadassah, the one yet to be revealed, to Norah and to Juniper, I realize that I have been given a constant reminder of how richly blessed I am to be your dad.

Kim, you have not always understood *why* getting an article out on Sunday night has been so important to me, yet you have always understood that it was important and that I *needed* to do it. Thank you for understanding. You have been a constant source of encouragement for my writings. Your words, which I think we first heard Katie speak to Hubble (*The Way We Were*), "I love the way you write" have meant and continue to mean more to me any book can ever say. The seasons of our life together have been seasons of incredible joy, overwhelming confusion, almost crippling pain and sorrow, and blessings beyond what we could have ever asked or imagined. Thank you for holding on with me, and to me, when neither of us knew what we were doing, what God was doing in and with us, and as we have waited for God to show us a clear path. Thank you for believing in me during those days and nights when I did not believe in myself. Thank you for forty-two years of believing that no matter what we face, we face it together, and that when we have lost or almost lost hope, we will keep moving forward *Until Hope Returns*. I love you.

Table of Contents

Introduction

In the mid to late 1990s as the World Wide Web and email communication were in the early stages of explosion, and the awareness of how powerful this electronic tool became more and more evident, I, along with multitudes of other Christian writers, began to realize that this new medium of communication should be used for good purposes. So, websites were developed, articles were shared via email and FAX, and some of us started writing what would become known as blogs. In early 1998, the first *A Norvell Note* was written and emailed to a small group of close friends.

Have you ever wondered what it was like to be one of the disciples who walked with Jesus during His short time on the earth? How would I react when He gathered the little children around Him? How I would have felt if one of the others got the seat next to Jesus at a meal? How did it feel when Jesus took the water and towel and washed my feet…my dirty feet? Would I have stood with Him when He was arrested? Where would I have been when He was being beaten and crucified?

I have wondered about those things. I still wonder about those things. I wonder more about how I will react while I am walking the earth with Jesus as my model. How will I treat those who are tired, broken, weak, sick, and struggling to get through life? How do I react when I am mistreated, when my dreams fade, and how will I handle the most difficult circumstances in my life? Will I remain faithful? Will I stand strong? Will I crumble under the pressure?

In *Until Hope Returns* I entertain some of those thoughts and share some examples of what I've seen, heard, and experienced. As much as anything, I try to offer hope where there is none, or where hope has been overshadowed by pain, disappointment, and loss. Drawn from everyday, ordinary life experiences, *Until Hope Returns* is a reminder that sometimes we have to smile through the tears, we have to endure the darkness of night in order to behold the beauty in a sunrise, and we have to hold on to the One who created us until hope returns to remind us that in Him is life…the abundant life.

Until Hope Returns is divided into four sections: Loving, Following, Hoping, and Reflecting. Each section begins with a theme verse of Scripture and a brief focus thought for that section.

You will discover as you read that during these twenty years I have experienced seasons of incredible joy (weddings, births, memorable vacations, and gatherings with family on holidays), and seasons of unspeakable sorrow (the death of loved ones, overwhelming heartbreak, and almost unbearable disappointments). There has been one constant throughout these years of joy and sorrow: the hope that I have because God is my Father and I am His child. His unrelenting presence and reckless love for me has sustained me, nourished me, and revived me during the difficult days and long nights when hope had diminished, and He's reminded me that He is always with me and will carry me if necessary until hope returns.

It is my hope that in these words you, too, will find real and lasting hope. If you are struggling with life and straining to hold to hope, or if you feel that all hope for better days is gone, you can hold on to Jesus until hope returns for you.

Part One
Loving

When you look at the life Jesus lived and watch Him closely, you realize that for Him life is about loving people. When asked, Jesus said the most important things are loving the Father and loving the Father's people. Jesus came to earth because He loved the world…the whole world. Loving like Jesus is not always easy, and it may not always be enjoyable, but it is the life of a follower of Jesus. Loving each other is the one true sign that we are His followers.

For God so loved the world that he gave his one and only Son, that whoever believes in him shall not perish but have eternal life. For God did not send his Son into the world to condemn the world, but to save the world through him.

John 3:16-18

My prayer is that God's love for you will inspire you to dream that one day you may be able to love like Jesus.

Jesus and Merle Haggard

When the news reported that Merle Haggard had died, not only was it a big story for the Nashville community, but for country music fans everywhere. Merle was truly a legend in country music.

His death prompted me to spend parts of the next couple of days listening to Merle's music. I listened in my car, in my office, and while walking the greenway. I was reminded of years long ago when as college students a friend and I would sit around with our guitars in "pickin' and a grinnin'" sessions which often included some of Merle's tunes. Our playlist often included: "Mama Tried," "White Line Fever," "Holding Things Together," "If We Make It Through December," and "Sing Me Back Home." As I listened to Merle's simple and easy tunes, I relived some of the times that also seemed, in retrospect, pretty simple and easy.

The more I listened, the more I began to see a connection between Jesus and Merle Haggard that I had never noticed.

The members of the church where I preach are reading through the New Testament together this year. Five chapters a week (Monday-Friday). Each Sunday we are using one of those texts for sermons, classes, and small group discussions. The reading for today is John 3. Reading ahead in preparation for this article I saw a connection between this well-known passage and the music of Merle Haggard.

For God so loved the world that he gave his one and only Son, that whoever believes in him shall not perish but have eternal life. For God did not send his Son into the world to condemn the world, but to save the world through him. – John 3:16-17

Merle sang songs about life. Many of his songs described a side of life that many followers of Jesus not only try to avoid, but spend considerable time condemning. For instance: "Working Man Blues," "The Fighting Side of Me," "I'm a Lonesome Fugitive," "Branded Man," "Ramblin Fever," and "I Threw Away the Rose." No doubt one of the reasons for Haggard's impact on the music world is that so many could relate to what he was singing.

Maybe you have felt, "If we make it through December (or to the end of the month, or next year, or through the holidays, or until we get paid) we'll be fine." Surely there have been days when you felt like you're just "Holding Things Together."

We, Jesus's people, sometimes like to put those kinds of stories in the category of what "those" people go through. "Good Godly people don't live like that." "Church goers don't have such hard times." "If they'd only get their life right and change their priorities, they wouldn't have so much trouble and heartache."

Jesus' words remind me that I'm missing the point when that is my attitude toward people. Jesus said, *"For God so loved the WORLD that he gave his one and only Son..."* Not only the good people. Not only the people who have life all together. Not only the good Christian people. God so loved the WORLD. People who don't have it all together, those who never seem to be able to get it all together, and those who at one time had it all together but failed miserably at keeping it together.

Jesus' words further convict my too often quick-to-judge attitude when He said, *"For God did not send his Son into the world to condemn the world, but to save the world through him."* Where did we get the idea that it is our job to condemn? Where did we get the impression that God could not handle His creation and needs us to step in and set things straight?

Merle Haggard sang from the heart about life. Sometimes life is hard, and then it gets worse. Sometimes we mess up; sometimes we get things right. Sometimes we feel like we are down and out, but we keep trying.

Jesus lived, died, and rose again to teach us to love the world like He loved the world. What if we loved the people Merle sang about like Jesus did? Maybe it is time we started.

The Sound of Dropping Stones

John 8 begins with the story (questionable whether it was actually included in the original text) of a trap set by "the teachers of the Law and the Pharisees" that involved a woman caught in the act of adultery being brought into the courtyard to stand judgment for her sin. Apparently not totally out of the ordinary, yet one has to wonder how often this was done since this was an opportune time for these religious leaders to put pressure on Jesus. (John 8:1-11)

Although it does not say in the text, surely at that moment when Jesus bent down and wrote on the ground for the second time, the only sounds in the temple courts area were those of stones dropping to the ground, the sniffling of the woman standing in front of Jesus, and the shuffling of feet as those, who moments earlier were ready to stone her, leave the courtyard.

Can you imagine how deafening that must have been? One moment she was humiliated and feared for her life. Then as the stones dropped she received another chance at life. Or, since we do not know her whole story, maybe this was really her first chance for a real life.

Expecting to feel the pain of the stones, instead she heard them drop to the ground, the silence, then the gentle loving voice of Jesus, "Woman, where are they? Has no one condemned you?" "Then neither do I condemn you. Go now and leave your life of sin."

Maybe as Jesus spoke to her, she opened her eyes and looked around to discover that the sound she heard really was that of stones dropping to the ground. As she wiped the tears from her eyes, or perhaps Jesus did, she began to see like she had never seen before. Instead of seeing a life of condemnation and shame, for the first time in a long time she saw a life of hope. For the first time, she felt the power of forgiveness. For the first time, instead of dreading the events of another day of being used, she began to think in terms of newness, refreshment, and kindness.

Jesus's stories give us the opportunity to ask, "Where I am I in this story?"

Like most of His stories, this one is aimed at those who held the stones in their hands. They have already passed judgment on this woman. She is yet again only an object to be used…this time by religion. They had no concern for her; only how she could be useful in catching Jesus in a misapplication of the Law. If you find yourself identifying with this group, maybe it is time you heard what that stone sounds like when your hand releases it and it drops to the ground.

Maybe you identify with the woman. You are guilty. The judgment waged against you is true and right. Whatever punishment the law demands is justified. Any feelings of value or self-worth left you long ago. The humiliation you feel as you stand there in the middle of the courtyard is only unique because you now stand there alone with Jesus. As you await His sentencing, you are stunned when instead of glaring eyes and painful stones, you hear His gentle voice ask about your accusers. When you acknowledge that they have departed, you are further stunned as you hear Him say, "Neither do I condemn you. Go and leave your life of sin."

Could this be happening? Could He possibly be forgiving me? Could this One they call Jesus actually be this loving, this gentle, this kind, this merciful?

Some will identify with the judgmental crowd; some will identify with the judged. It is my hope that we will strive to identify with Jesus and develop a spirit more like His. Not as a judge; though, He certainly could have judged her. Not as one who condemns; though, He could have condemned her. May we strive to be one who loves gently, judges rightly, and forgives completely!

Known by Our Love

A new command I give you: Love one another. As I have loved you, so you must love one another. By this everyone will know that you are my disciples, if you love one another. – John 13:34-35

"Love one another." Sounds easy enough. Just love each other. That is how people will know that we are Jesus's disciples. Just love each other.

You do not need any title. You do not need to pay a membership fee. There are no hoops to jump through. You do not need any special marking or identification badge. You do not need to make a loud public announcement about being a follower of Jesus. Just love one another.

Churches who bear the name of Jesus Christ: Love one another. Churches who disagree on some doctrinal beliefs: Love one another. Churches who have almost nothing in common except your love for Jesus: Love one another. Churches that disagree on the specifics of what should be preached from your pulpits, the specifics of how you should worship, but agree on Whom you worship: Love one another.

As you live within your churches, you really need to love one another. Your roles are different, so love one another. Your gifts are different, so love one another. You may differ on the exact way ministry should be carried out, so love one another. There are going to be times some people really get on your nerves, so love one another.

Love one another. That is how everyone will know that you are my disciples. Sounds easy. It is easy as long as everyone stays in their designated places doing what they are supposed to do. It is easy as long as nobody tries to do anything that goes against what I am comfortable with. It is easy until I am not getting my way, or it appears that I am not getting my way. It is easy to love one another as long as we think alike, dress alike, and talk alike.

Those times when life gets stressful are the times Jesus probably had in mind when He said, "Love one another." He knew His disciples were about to experience stress, distress, danger, and confusion unlike anything

6

they had ever known. He knew they were going to be tested in their faith and devotion and would be tempted to turn against and away from each other. He knew that the world would be watching them as they endured the images of Jesus on the cross and in the tomb. He knew they would need one another more in the future than they had in the previous three years. So, He told them, "Love one another."

Jesus knew the challenges that disciples of His day would be facing as the cross loomed closer. He also knows the challenges disciples in our day are facing as we attempt to live faithfully in our times of stress, distress, danger, and confusion. He knows our faith will be tested and that we will be tempted to turn against and away from each other. He knows that our world will be watching us as we endure difficult times. He knows we will need one another more and more as we wait for the Lord's return. He knows, so He still tells us, "Love one another."

Sounds like it should be easy. Whether it is easy or not, He wants us to love one another so that everyone will know we are His disciples because of the love we have for one another. He still wants us to be known by our love.

Gas Prices, Politics, the Weather, and Jesus

Gas prices change at irregular intervals. There seems to be no rhyme or reason to the changes. Gas prices go up and go down, sometimes multiple times during a twenty-four period. In our area, you can drive down the road and the price of gas will fluctuate as much as ten cents higher or lower. This varies from week to week, depending on which location you go to. If a gas line is ruptured in Alabama, the price of gas in some areas near us will go up, and some will not. Economists try to predict what will happen with gas prices, and sometimes they are right, and sometimes they are not. There seems to be little consistency.

Politics is as inconsistent as gas prices. Whoever is in a position of leadership determines the protestors and the supporters. The amount of power of the president is dependent upon which political party has control of the other branches of government. Even then, it seems that the bill he signs or does not sign can cause a shift in those who are supporters and those who are considered the opposition. Political analysts try to predict how politicians will act or react and how the constituents will respond. Sometimes they are right, and sometimes they are not. There seems to be little consistency.

The weather, particularly during this season, is almost impossible to predict. We get frustrated with, amused with, and sympathetic towards those who have the task of making accurate predictions. Temperatures on some winter days are more like early spring or late fall. Predictions of light snow are overturned with a slight shift in the jet stream that produces several inches (and of course global warming must also be factored in). Predictions of heavy snow excite children, only to disappoint them when the jet streams move just a degree or two in one direction or another. Forecasters, using all of their advanced technologies, do their best to make predictions that are as accurate as possible, sometimes they are exactly right, and sometimes they are not. There seems to be little consistency.

Jesus! Ahhh, Jesus! Jesus is someone who you can know, with absolute certainty, is consistent. We can consistently depend on Jesus. Jesus offers us something solid to hold on to. Jesus provides us with a tangible understanding of consistency. The writer of Hebrews encourages the followers who were weary of the inconsistencies of living the holy life in a very hostile world with these words. *Jesus Christ is the same yesterday and today and forever. Do not be carried away by all kinds of strange teachings.* – Hebrews 13:8,9a

Sometime today I will fill my car up with gas. Before I go, I will check an app on my phone to see who has the cheapest price in my area.

Several times within the next twenty-four hours, I will get updates on all my devices or scan comments on social media that are giving details and opinions on the latest decisions coming out of the White House.

Before I leave the house, I will check the weather to see if there will be rain, sunshine, or clouds.

The sources that provide me with information about gas prices, politics, and the weather are useful and as dependable as *humanly* possible. I am blessed to have these many tools at my fingertips to help make life more predictable and easier to manage.

Jesus, however, is always on target. His Word is always right. His predictions of what will happen to those who follow Him are true. His projections for those who do not follow Him are solid. He is never surprised by the price of gas, the actions of politicians, the weather, or anything else that happens in our world. When we turn to Him for direction, for wisdom, and for strength, He always comes through with exactly what we need.

As you face the inconsistencies of day-to-day life, use whatever is available to help you live the best life you can live. But more than anything or anyone else, keep your eyes and your heart focused on Jesus. He is the one you can depend on all of the time. "He is the same yesterday and today and forever."

Therefore, since we are surrounded by such a great cloud of witnesses, let us throw

off everything that hinders and the sin that so easily entangles. And let us run with perseverance the race marked out for us, fixing our eyes on Jesus, the pioneer and perfecter of faith. For the joy set before him he endured the cross, scorning its shame, and sat down at the right hand of the throne of God. Consider him who endured such opposition from sinners, so that you will not grow weary and lose heart. – Hebrews 12:1-3

Every Shot is Important

I noticed something while watching the professional golfers recently. They play every shot as if it were the most important shot of the tournament. Not just the crucial putts. Not just the drive on the narrow fairway. But they play every shot like they could win or lose the tournament based upon that one shot. After that shot, regardless of the outcome, they go through the same pre-shot routine on the next shot. I suppose that is one reason they play better than I do. It also teaches an important lesson about life: Every shot is important.

I realize that every event of every day does not have life or death consequences. I know that every decision we make does not affect where we will spend eternity. And I know that every conversation we have does not have to be serious and profound. But what if we viewed every action in life as an opportunity to do the absolute very best we could? What if we treated even the very mundane daily routines as if they make the world a better place?

Instead of just another phone call from a friend, we could have a talk about life, about what is really important, and we could share our dreams and listen to theirs. No more chit-chat or idle words. Our words would become words of life, not just words. Every conversation is important.

Instead of just another meal with the family, we could truly share a mealtime with our family. We could hear what kind of day they had, and really care. We could laugh more. We could actually enjoy the food and be grateful for it, but the food would not be the focus. Every meal is important.

Instead of just another sunrise or sunset, we could actually see them as another day full of opportunities in which to share the beauty of the Creator. We could see them as the beginning and the ending of another twenty-four-hour gift from God. Every day is important.

Instead of just another person, we could see people as human beings with needs, emotions, feelings, and lives to share. We would not disregard

11

people so often. We would not ignore people so easily. We could actually take time to get to know them, listen to them, share what is good about life, and encourage them. Every person is important.

Instead of just another church service, we could see the gathering of the saints as a time to rejoice and be glad that we have comfortable places to worship, a time with fellow strugglers on our journey, and a time with brothers and sisters who share the greatest bond of all. We could enter the presence of God with a reverent anticipation for what He wants to share with us and what we can offer to Him. Every assembly is important.

Instead of just another relationship, we could view our mate, our child, our parent, our friend, our work associate, even that guy down the street who we know only as that guy down the street as one of God's creations. They are not here to simply occupy space any more than we are. They have a purpose. They have a soul. They have a heart. Every relationship is important.

In 2 Corinthians 5:16 Paul said, *So from now on we regard no one from a worldly point of view.* In Ephesians 5:15-16 he said, *Be very careful, then, how you live – not as unwise but as wise, making the most of every opportunity, because the days are evil.* His approach to life seemed to be such that every day and every act was something to be valued and treated with an appropriate amount of seriousness.

Treating every golf shot as the most important of the day will no doubt extend your time on the course (and may irritate your playing partners or those playing behind you), but who knows, it might improve your game. Treating the people in your life and the events in your life as important will also take more time and may require more of you. But the results will be worth it – if not in this life, then certainly in the next.

Enjoy every shot – it is important.

You May Never Know

You may never know what good you are doing when you take time to visit that friend who really needed someone to listen to her. You may never know, but because you took the time to listen she was able to get through a crisis, and many more since then, and now she is listening to the heart of others. You may never know, but keep listening.

You may never know how important it was for you to show a special interest in that student who sat quietly in your classroom and seldom participated in the class discussions. You may never know, but because you showed your concern he is now teaching in his own classroom and keeping a watchful eye for that student who needs some special attention. You may never know, but keep expressing your concern.

You may never know what a difference it made for you to be with that family when their mother passed away. All you did was take a bucket of chicken, asked what they needed, and washed a few dishes. But because you took the time to demonstrate your concern, that family makes sure when they hear of a family who has lost a loved one that there is a bucket of chicken and someone to wash a few dishes. You may never know, but keep doing those little things you do.

You may never know how significant it was for you to leave your home, travel to that strange land, eat strange food, and share your faith with those people you had never met. You may never know, but because you did, one of those people who heard you share your faith is now sharing his. You may never know, but keep going, and keep sharing your faith.

You may never know what an impact you had when you left work early so you could attend your son's basketball game. You may never know, but because you did take the time to show him he was more important than a bigger salary, he is now leaving work early so he can enjoy his son's game. You may never know, but leave work and go to the game anyway.

13

You may never know what impression you made when you told that person you work with that you were praying for him as he was going through a particularly difficult time with his family. You may never know, but because you prayed and told him you were praying, he was able to hold on and survive the crisis. You may never know, but keep praying.

Jesus talked a lot about the importance of doing little things like giving a cup of cold water to someone who was thirsty, visiting the sick and imprisoned, planting a seed, and being kind to the "little ones." You may never know, but please never stop doing those little things. You may never know, then again you may.

Enjoy planting the seed.

And They Lived Happily Ever After

My wife has been commenting on and recommending a book (*Turn Toward the Wind* by Dale Hanson Bourke) to people for almost two years. I finally worked my way through my "Books-I-Need-to-Read" list to begin reading it last week. I was still in the introduction when I read this sentence: "The Bible does not contain the phrase, 'And they lived happily ever after.'" (Bourke, Dale Hanson. *Turn Toward the Wind*. Zondervan, 1995.) I have known that to be true for a long time but have never seen it stated quite like that. Now, as we ring in the New Year, those words ring in my ears.

The words are ringing because I am thinking of a couple that pledged to love each other forever as they stood in front of the gathering of friends and family. Then things changed. The relationship was no longer fun. Saying "I love you" became more and more difficult. Feeling it seemed to be impossible. He found someone else. They did not live happily ever after.

The words stand out to me because I am reminded of the guy who landed the job of his dreams. He was at the pinnacle of his career. He was the envy of his colleagues. He was the bright star on the horizon. Then he made one mistake that destroyed it all. He is not living happily ever after.

The words remind me of the couple that dreamed of being parents. They waited for years. They had it all planned, and everything was worked out. Except they had not planned on her having complications in her pregnancy. Then the baby girl, born much earlier than expected, had internal problems that required several surgeries. Medical bills piled up. She got worse. She died. They continue to live, but not happily.

I see the truth of those words when I think of the group of believers who started out with a vision of ministry and a confidence that God would bless their efforts. But growth was slow. Egos grew. People became exclusive and possessive. They developed a fear of change. The Spirit was quenched. They continue to exist, but it seems like forever since they were happy.

Bourke concludes the introduction with these words: *See, I am doing a new thing! Now it springs up; do you not perceive it? I am making a way in the desert and streams in the wasteland.* – Isaiah 43:19

Life may not be turning out as you had expected. When the calendar changed a year ago you never imagined you could get in such a mess in only twelve months. Your life is not anything like you planned. You are hurting. You are tired. You are confused. You are not sure how much more you can handle. This is not the "happily ever after" fairy tale that you had envisioned. You are ready to quit.

It is true, sometimes they do not live happily ever after. But before you give up, remember God's words: "See, I am doing a new thing!" He has something planned. It is a new year. He is doing a new thing.

Enjoy the new thing...whatever it is.

When I Grow Up

During the preschool graduation program the teacher read a brief biography of each child. Included in each statement was the child's plan for the future. One wants to be a doctor. Another wants to be a nurse. One wants to be a teacher. One wants to drive race cars. One wants to decorate for parties. Three or four want to be policemen or firemen. One wants to do nothing. And one wants to be a mom.

As I watched the young graduates accept their diplomas and applause from the adoring crowd of parents, grandparents, aunts, and uncles, I remembered some of my dreams. Some have now come true. And some have not. No doubt the same will be true for these youngsters as they move through their lives.

With many of those childhood dreams now far from my grasp, I find that my dreams have changed. I no longer dream of playing basketball for the Boston Celtics or winning the World Series with the New York Yankees. Being rich seldom occupies much of my time, and spending the night in the White House will probably only happen when my son becomes President. But I still have a dream.

My dream is that I will be more like Jesus today than I was yesterday and less today than I will be tomorrow. Like many of the other dreams, this one sometimes seems well beyond my reach. As I try and fail to make the mark, I wonder if I will ever make it. In fact, there are days when I wonder if I have made any progress at all. Still I dream. I want to be like Him.

I want to love like Him. I want to listen like Him. I want to teach like Him. I want to respond like Him. I want to be the kind of husband He would be, the kind of father He would be, the kind of friend He would be, and the kind of preacher He would be. I want to live like He lived, and die like He died knowing I have given my all. That is what I want to be.

What would you like to be when you grow up?

The First Step

If you drive about forty-five minutes from our house to the top of Lookout Mountain then head toward the West Brow, you can find a place where hang gliders practice their sport. We go there occasionally to watch, not to jump. Every time we go I think about how exciting it must be to leave the top of the mountain, sail over the valley, and land in the green field across the valley.

The last time we were there the man in charge asked my wife and I if we would like to try it. "No thanks," I said. "I'd love to experience what it feels like once you are airborne and gliding in the breeze, but that first step would kill me." He laughed a little, then proceeded to tell us that by the time you get to the point where you could leave the platform you have received so much training that that first step is not nearly as scary as it is appears. I told him that made sense, but I still declined his offer.

Even though I understand his point and know the training could make the difference between being an interested observer and a bold jumper, it is still hard for me to imagine what it would be like to take that first step off the platform. Because of that fear (I like to think there is some wisdom in that decision as well), chances are I will never know the thrill of flight or the exhilaration of the experience. That first step is just too much to overcome.

The same thing happens to us sometimes when we look across the valley of life at all there is to enjoy, all there is to know, and all there is to experience. We want the joy, we want the knowledge, and we want the experience, but quite often that first step keeps us from taking that leap of faith. Some people will never marry because they are afraid of that first step. Some people will marry but never experience a really fulfilling relationship with their mate because they are afraid of that first step of opening up and sharing their heart. Some people will never experience true friendship because they are afraid to take that first step into the world of relationships. Some people will never know real fulfillment in their work because they prefer to remain where they are and dream of what

18

could be instead of taking that first step toward leaving what is familiar and comfortable. Some people will never know the abundant life God has planned for them because that first step of faith is too frightening.

Hebrews 11:1 says, *Now faith is being sure of what we hope for and certain of what we do not see.*

Before the hang glider takes the first step off the platform at the top of the mountain, he must be certain that the wind is right even though he cannot see the wind. He must be sure that his gear is right and that his training will keep him safe. Being confident of those things, he can leap from the platform and smile with the wind in his face as he glides across the valley.

Before a person commits his life to God he must be sure of one thing: God is there. That's all the training he needs to take that first step. Once that first step is taken the abundant life will begin.

The rewards are there for all who are willing to take the first step. Are you on the platform watching, wondering, wishing, hoping, dreaming? Is God asking you to take that first step toward Him?

To stand and watch while others hang glide is enough for me. To watch while others experience the joys of a relationship with the Father is not acceptable. The first step can be tough, but He is there to carry you as you fly and to make sure the landing will be safe.

Take the first step.

Do It Right

Whatever you do, work at it with all your heart, as working for the Lord, not for men, since you know that you will receive an inheritance from the Lord as a reward. It is the Lord Christ you are serving. – Colossians 3:23,24

When I read that passage, the phrase that comes to mind is: "Do it right!" What a difference it would make if we could apply that principle in our daily walk.

If we did what we do with all our heart in the workplace, our work would likely be of much higher quality. Nothing shoddy around this office. No room for a halfhearted effort in this stockroom. No place for mediocrity in dealing with these customers. There would likely be nothing but first-rate, high quality work if we would do it with all our might.

If we did what we do with all our heart as working for the Lord, we would be more careful how we treated people. We would be more concerned about quality, not quantity. We would spend more time listening and less time giving orders. We would be even more tired at the end of the day, but there would be more fulfillment in our fatigue.

If we did what we do with all our heart as working for the Lord, not for men, we would spend less time looking over our shoulder and more time looking into our heart. We would worry less about keeping our job and spend more time improving our job. We would be less concerned about the amount of the paycheck and more concerned about inheritance being prepared for us.

If we did what we do with all our heart as working for the Lord, not for men, knowing we have a reward from the Lord waiting for us, we would surely tell more people about the One who provides the reward. We would surely express our gratitude more freely to those we love. We would feel less pressure about the right performance and more interested in performing right.

If we did what we do with all our heart as working for the Lord, we would not be as concerned about who is watching, who is listening, and who gets the glory. We would give Him the glory for all that we do, and do all we could to give Him the glory.

With those kinds of results at our disposal, let's make a commitment to do it right this week. Remember who you work for. Whatever you do, do it with all your heart.

Do it right!

With All Your Heart

I have always been drawn to people who give it their whole heart. No matter what the "it" is, I like it when they give it their all. Singers who sing with passion. Actors who give the role they're playing all their energy. Athletes who leave it all on the field, court, or course. Children who sing with all their heart. Teachers who teach because they have a passion for sharing knowledge. Preachers who preach because they have a passion for sharing God with their listeners. Churches that serve the people of their community with joy and enthusiasm.

On the other hand, I am easily frustrated with and completely turned off by those who do things halfheartedly. Houses that get half-built are not very impressive. Movies that are done poorly. Games that are played without a desire for excellence. Music that has no life to it. Worship that is not really worship.

I like people and things that are done with the whole heart. I get down on myself when I slip into a mode of doing things halfway. Articles that are written just to get something written. Books that are read just to get to the end. Sermons that are preached without the Spirit. Conversations that do not lead to life.

I am talking about more than enthusiasm. Anyone can act enthusiastically. I am talking about wholehearted devotion. I like to do things with my whole heart, see things done with the whole heart, be a part of things that are done with the whole heart, and be with people who want to give their whole heart to their task. I am not saying I always give my whole heart, but with all my heart I want to grow to the point that nothing is done halfway.

How do I get there? What do I need to learn, or relearn, that will help me to live my life with my whole heart? Here are three passages that remind me that I need to give my whole heart.

One of the teachers of the law came and heard them debating. Noticing that Jesus had given them a good answer, he asked him, "Of all the commandments, which is the most important?"

"The most important one," answered Jesus, "is this: `Hear, O Israel, the Lord our God, the Lord is one. Love the Lord your God with all your heart and with all your soul and with all your mind and with all your strength.' The second is this: `Love your neighbor as yourself.' There is no commandment greater than these." – Mark 12:28-31

Whatever you do, work at it with all your heart, as working for the Lord, not for men, since you know that you will receive an inheritance from the Lord as a reward. It is the Lord Christ you are serving. Anyone who does wrong will be repaid for his wrong, and there is no favoritism. – Colossians 3:23-25

These are the words of the Amen, the faithful and true witness, the ruler of God's creation. I know your deeds, that you are neither cold nor hot. I wish you were either one or the other! So, because you are lukewarm—neither hot nor cold—I am about to spit you out of my mouth. –Revelation 3:14-16

I look forward to the day when I give my whole heart to everything I do. When I write, I will put my whole heart into the piece of literature. When I preach, I will put my whole heart into the sermon. When I listen, I will give my whole heart to the person speaking. When I worship, I will give my whole heart to the Lord. I am not there yet, but I am working on it. I want to live with my whole heart. I hope you will give your whole heart to the Lord.

With all my heart.

Fading Dreams

A football team steps onto the field with confidence and a firm conviction that victory is certain. Images of celebrating in the end zone fill their minds. By the end of the first quarter those dreams are fading and all but gone. A mishandled punt, a fumbled hand-off, and an interception – by the end of the first quarter the deficit seems insurmountable.

Every professional golfer begins the Thursday round visualizing what it will feel like to stand on the eighteenth green on Sunday knowing that victory has been achieved. A miserable front nine, an even worse back nine, and the professional feels the tournament slipping away. By late Friday afternoon the car is packed, the dream of victory is gone, and thoughts of "maybe next week" fill his thinking.

The season begins with every college coach thinking, "This could be our year." The early part of the season goes well with victories coming easy and often. An injury to a key player, the chemistry of the team changes, and the victories stop coming. Dreams of championships and celebrations become thoughts of what might have been…if only.

The enterprising businessman has dreams of independence, exotic vacations, and an early retirement. Plans are made. Facilities are acquired. Finances are secured. The business opens. Excitement is in the air and things look good…for a while. The customers simply do not come. Bills pile up. Discouragement sets in. What began as the dream of a lifetime ends with disappointment and disillusionment.

The couple stands before the audience of friends and family with their life all planned. "We'll get married, we'll both work for a while, we'll have children, then grandchildren, and we'll live happily ever after." A year or two into the marriage the excitement fades, the romance seems to be gone, he never talks, she is always angry.

The couple had dreamed of retirement days filled with travel and leisure time together and visiting the children and grandchildren. Then he got sick. Then he was gone. Now, she's alone.

The small group of college friends had a dream of mission work in a distant land. They receive the training. They find the field of work. They accumulate the operating funds. They enjoy a royal send-off. The first few years are glorious. Joy in service. There is significant positive fruit from their labors. A division occurs. Egos are damaged. Pride gets in the mix. The mission ends, and friendships are lost.

Sometimes dreams fade quickly. Sometimes dreams fade slowly. Sometimes dreams come true. Sometimes we wait for God to work His plan to show us things beyond our wildest dreams.

At a point in the history of God's people when their dreams seemed to be fading, the Lord spoke to Joshua, their new leader in Joshua 1:1-11:

After the death of Moses, the servant of the LORD, the LORD said to Joshua son of Nun, Moses' aide: "Moses my servant is dead. Now then, you and all these people, get ready to cross the Jordan River into the land I am about to give to them — to the Israelites. I will give you every place where you set your foot, as I promised Moses. Your territory will extend from the desert to Lebanon, and from the great river, the Euphrates — all the Hittite country — to the Great Sea on the west. No one will be able to stand up against you all the days of your life. As I was with Moses, so I will be with you; I will never leave you nor forsake you.

"Be strong and courageous, because you will lead these people to inherit the land I swore to their forefathers to give them. Be strong and very courageous. Be careful to obey all the law my servant Moses gave you; do not turn from it to the right or to the left, that you may be successful wherever you go. Do not let this Book of the Law depart from your mouth; meditate on it day and night, so that you may be careful to do everything written in it. Then you will be prosperous and successful. Have I not commanded you? Be strong and courageous. Do not be terrified; do not be discouraged, for the LORD your God will be with you wherever you go."

So, Joshua ordered the officers of the people: "Go through the camp and tell the people, 'Get your supplies ready. Three days from now you will cross the Jordan here to go in and take possession of the land the LORD your God is giving you for your own.'"

Is your dream fading? Do you sense it is about to disappear? Has your dream already faded? Hear the Lord: "Be strong and courageous . . . get ready . . . I will be with you; I will never leave you nor forsake you . . . Be strong and courageous."

Faded dreams can be reborn. Get ready. God is still God.

New Things

See, the former things have taken place, and new things I declare; before they spring into being I announce them to you. – Isaiah 42:9

Decorations are coming down. Wrapping paper is being packed away and stored. Neighborhoods are darker. Parties are over. Gifts have been given and some exchanged. Resolutions are being made and some broken. Vacations are ending. Diets are beginning and ending. The old year has gone. The new year has come. It is time for new things.

No one knows the new things that will come our way during the course of the next twelve months, but one thing is certain: new things will come.

Think about the last twelve months. Reflect on the new things you have seen Him do in your life during the past year. Think of the new people you have met during the last year. Think about the new experiences you have had. Think about the songs you have heard and learned. Think about the new books that have been written you have read. Think about the new movies that have been released you have seen.

This year will also be filled with new things. New opportunities in your work place will come. New opportunities to enrich your family life will come. Many new things are sure to appear on the horizon relating to your career and your relationships.

New things will come in your spiritual walk. As you enter into this New Year, if you will open your heart to God and ask Him to show you what He wants you to do, who He wants you to be, where He wants to take you, He will do it. He will show you new things.

Look for the new things the Lord wants to show you. Stay alert. Listen to Him as He speaks new things to you. Watch for the new things He will do that will amaze you. Open your eyes to what the Lord has planned for you.

The Lord wants to show you new things. New babies. New friends. New Christians. New worship experiences. New insights. New revelations. New dreams. New hopes. New goals. New games.

The next twelve months promise all kinds of new things. Athletes will set new goals and reach them. Teachers will see students acquire new knowledge. Golfers will play new courses and hit new shots. Preachers will preach new sermons. Families will move into new homes. Husbands and wives will reach new dimensions in their relationships.

You have heard these things; look at them all. Will you not admit them? From now on I will tell you of new things, of hidden things unknown to you. — Isaiah 48:6

Let God tell you of new things.

Dare to Dream

As I write this I am actually sitting in the living room floor of what appears will be our next house. It is completely empty. It has been empty for several months. Empty, that is, except for a few appliances, light fixtures, a few dead flies, and piles of dirt and dust left behind by the previous owners. I have visions of what could be. This could be the place where we will entertain guests, receive visitors, share dinners, hosts parties, take naps, laugh, cry, pray, study the Bible, sing, and play with our grandchildren.

I have moved to a new place of ministry. I'm listening to people talk of how things used to be, how they are now, and how they wish things could be. Some are reluctant to talk about the future because of the pain of the past. Together we are developing a vision of what could be. We are trying to remain open to what God has in store for us. We dream of growing spiritually and as a result of that growing numerically. We are dreaming of sharing the message of love, hope, mercy, peace, and grace with our community.

Within the week our daughter will turn eighteen years of age, and within the month she will head off to college. She is ready. She is excited. She is looking forward to what God reveals as His vision for her. She is dreaming of adventure, of learning, of fun, and of experiencing all that the college years offer.

Also, within the week our son will get married. He, his soon-to-be wife, and both mothers have made (and are continuing to make) major plans for the rehearsal dinner, the special wedding events, the ceremony, and the reception. The two of them have prepared for this day mentally, spiritually, educationally, and physically. The two of them have dreamed of this day (and night) for years. They have visions and dreams of their future as a family.

Every day we wake up to new possibilities, new opportunities, and new challenges. Do we dare to dream of what could be? Are we willing to run the risk of being disappointed? Are we ready for what will happen if the dreams don't come true? Is it worth the risk?

Perhaps the more important questions are: Can we afford not to dream? Is that worth the risk of never seeing dreams come true? Is the safety of not dreaming better than the thrill of experiencing a dream come true? Would we really want to live a life without dreams?

Consider these words of Jesus:

"Because you have so little faith. I tell you the truth, if you have faith as small as a mustard seed, you can say to this mountain, 'Move from here to there' and it will move. Nothing will be impossible for you." – Matthew 17:20

"With man this is impossible, but with God all things are possible." – Matthew 19:26

"With man this is impossible, but not with God; all things are possible with God." – Mark 10:27

"What is impossible with man is possible with God." – Luke 18:27

Don't ever be afraid to dream. With God, dreams can come true.

Part Two
Following

Living like Jesus means living in abundance. Don't equate abundance with good health, endless wealth, and incomparable success. Instead, think fullness. A life lived in and for Jesus is a life lived in fullness. The life of a Jesus disciple means being full of love, joy, peace, patience, kindness, goodness, faithfulness, gentleness, and self-control.

The thief comes only to steal and kill and destroy; I have come that they may have life and have it to the full.
John 10:10

My prayer is that you begin, or continue, to live like Jesus and that you experience all the fullness that He has planned for you.

Habits that Haunt Us

As I was reading Mark's account of the events just prior to the crucifixion of Jesus Christ, I noticed some things that I had never noticed before about the process that led up to that horrible death of our Lord. In chapter fifteen when Jesus was brought before the powers that were for questioning and judgement, He remained silent, which amazed Pilate. The mockery of a trial extends to the crowd that had gathered for the show. Verse 6 explains that there had been a custom at such occasions to release the prisoners that the crowd requested. As Pilate wrestled with the decision, the crowd asked Pilate ...*to do for them what he usually did* (Mark 15:8).

Sometimes our habits come back to haunt us. Sometimes, like the voices from the crowd surrounding Pilate, our habits call out to us saying, "Do for us what you usually do." Maybe you have been haunted by some of your habits.

You have made up your mind that you are going to treat people differently. The sermon you just heard convicted you that a change was in order. You are determined. On your way home from the assembly, your wife asks you to stop at the "convenience" store for a package of rolls for lunch. No big deal. A quick dash in, grab the rolls, back in the car, and you'll still get home before the kick-off. Who could have known there would be a line in front of you in the "convenience" store? Three people are buying lottery tickets — two can't decide which game to play; one cannot find his credit card. The fourth person, a small child, discovers she does not have enough money to pay for the super-duper-huge-gulp she has spilt all over the floor as she made her way to the counter. She ends up going out to the car for more money. Do you hear the crowd calling? "Do for us what you usually do. Chew them out! Tell them what you really think about their business! Let them know that you will never step foot in this store as long as you live! And while you are at it, save a little for your wife who made you stop here in the first place! That's it. Do for us what you usually do."

You have managed to get into a bad situation at work in which you have to compromise a few of your convictions. No big deal. Just shifting a few figures around here and there. No one will ever notice. It's just a little lie. Then the stakes get higher. You know what you should do, but you hear the crowd. "Do for us what you usually do. Go ahead, change the figures. Alter the wording. Make it sound better than it really is. No one will get hurt. No one will know. No one will care. Do for us what you usually do."

Your language has become a little salty. Words your parents would never have used, nor approved of your using, have become fairly common in your vocabulary. You have tried to justify them by explaining that the times are different, and that a lot of your friends use much worse language than you do. But still you know it's not right. So, you make up your mind to stop it. Almost before you get the thought planted in your head, your software program flashes a message about some %^&*$ error. In addition to the message on the screen, you see a message from the crowd. "Do for us what you usually do. Spew those words. Let 'em fly! You're frustrated. It's okay. It's just a word. Do for us what you usually do."

Your choice of programs has changed over the last few months. Some of them, many of them, are not appropriate. Some are down-right raunchy. You know it. You know the Lord knows it. But the acting is good, and somewhere in there is a good message. Besides, it doesn't affect you. Hear the crowd? "Do for us what you usually do. Keep on watching. It's gonna get better sooner or later. Do for us what you usually do."

Your temper has gotten you into trouble more times than you care to remember. It's time to get a handle on it. Never again. It's under control. You are determined not to lose your cool. But before you can turn around, someone has done something so incredibly stupid you simply cannot resist. Then you hear the crowd. "Do for us what you usually do. Don't hold back. Blow them away! Do for us what you usually do."

Habits do haunt us. Just about the time we think we have broken ourselves of that horrible addiction – boom! It's back. Stronger. More tempting. More in control than ever. The crowd screams louder than we have ever heard them.

Do you suppose when Pilate heard the crowd chanting, "Do for us what you usually do," he wished he had never gotten into the habit of releasing the prisoner requested by the crowd? Do you suppose he wished he had never relinquished that segment of his power? Perhaps his old habit was coming back to haunt him. He could have done it differently. We can, too. It won't be easy to go against the crowd. We may have to silence the crowd.

To get rid of the habits that haunt us, we may need to listen to someone other than the crowd. *No temptation has seized you except what is common to man. And God is faithful; he will not let you be tempted beyond what you can bear. But when you are tempted, he will also provide a way out so that you can stand up under it.* – 1 Corinthians 10:13

Enjoy a new habit.

Making Something Out of Nothing

While recuperating from a recent surgery about all I felt like doing was sitting in my recliner or sleeping. When I was awake, I spent some time scanning our sixty-seven cable TV channels for some worthwhile viewing on daytime television. I didn't find much. Finally, I found something to challenge my interest: "The Three Stooges" (much to the displeasure of my wife). This episode found Moe, Curly, and Larry in business at the Pip Brothers Tailor Shop and Cleaners. Larry was baffled by a spot on his pants. He rubbed and scratched and fumed until he finally rubbed a large hole in the pants, only to discover that the spot was actually a ray of light coming through the window. I laughed at his ridiculous behavior and realized the appeal of this brand of comedy is the ability of these three (and others like them) to take a simple task and turn it into an incredibly complicated venture. The humor comes in being reminded of my own successful efforts of making something out of nothing.

There was the time my car would not start. I had to have the car towed to the dealership so a mechanic could locate and replace one little wire. The final cost to have a twenty-seven-cent wire replaced was nearly $50.

Then there was the time I was going to repair our old television set. I got a great deal on it right before we were married. Did you know that if you touch the wrong wire on the back of a television you can get quite a shock?

Once, in our first year of marriage, we had the opportunity to go to Hawaii. Two people going to Hawaii for five days. We carried enough clothes to cover most of the people on Waikiki Beach (some of them could have used it, but that's beside the point). Something simple turned into something really complicated.

Maybe I'm not the only one who has made something out of nothing. Maybe you have been in a situation where someone said, "Hey, let's get a group together and go out for dinner. Nothing fancy. Just a fun night out." Simple enough, right? Wrong! Before you knew it, there was this big hassle about where you would go, whom you should invite, what you should wear, what you would order when you got there, and whether you would have dessert there or go somewhere else. Nothing turned into something.

What about the holidays? Most holidays were originally designed either to simply honor a person, or set aside as a time of remembrance and celebration. How did they ever become such major events? Christmas, for instance, as I understand it, is supposed to be an observance of the birth of the baby Jesus, but it has turned into a budget-busting extravaganza producing stress, anxiety, and competition to see who can get or give the most expensive gifts. Something simple turned into something complicated.

Tried to have a "simple" vacation lately? You have a week off. The kids are out of school. You want to go someplace that will be relaxing and fun for the whole family. Sounds like a great idea. By the end of the week you are worn out from traveling, sick of eating out, tired of each other, and wondering what happened to the fun and relaxation. Oh, did I forget to mention that everyone caught a stomach virus?

Church people are sometimes guilty of making something out of nothing. Someone has an idea for a ministry. "Sounds good. Permission granted. Go for it!" Someone else objects. Someone else has a better idea. Someone else gets jealous. Some get their feelings hurt because they were not asked to participate. Some others pout because their opinions were not considered. Before long you drop your idea. Can anyone remember whom it was we were trying to help in the first place? We made something out of nothing.

We don't always have control over how complicated things get. I recall hearing a doctor ask me a few years ago, "When are you going to have your teeth fixed?" Sounded simple enough. Nearly four years of orthodontic and dental work and three surgeries later, we are almost there. We can even find humor in things like that. (I can laugh about it...now!)

God encountered similar complications. His idea? "I'll send My one and only Son into the world to show the people how much I love them." Sounds like a good plan. Some resented it. Some wouldn't believe it. Some rebelled against it. Some ignored it. Some simply accepted it. Some kept adding to the requirements until it became quite complicated to accept His invitation.

We can laugh as we watch comedians get themselves in all kinds of ridiculous predicaments and struggle for a resolution. We can even laugh when we see ourselves portrayed in comical scenarios. I suppose, at times, we all may make things much more complicated than they were intended to be. That is okay when it involves cleaning a pair of pants, or packing boxes on a conveyer belt, or trying to take five or six dogs for a walk at the same time. It is not nearly so funny when it involves one's soul.

Have you allowed your relationship with the Lord to become too complicated because you are trying to follow everyone's rules and regulations? Have you lost the joy in your relationship with Christ because someone keeps telling you it is not as simple as following Jesus? The simple truth is: God has made something from nothing by inviting us, in our hopeless and helpless condition, to become a part of His Body. Let's not mess with it.

Oh, that spot on those pants? You better check. It might just be the light shining through the window.

Enjoy life's humor.

Words

As a child I learned, "Sticks and stones may break my bones, but words will never hurt me."

Now, I read Jesus' words, *"You're familiar with the command to the ancients, 'Do not murder.' I'm telling you that anyone who is so much as angry with a brother or sister is guilty of murder. Carelessly call a brother 'idiot!' and you just might find yourself hauled into court. Thoughtlessly yell 'stupid' at a sister and you are on the brink of hellfire. The simple moral fact is that words kill."* (Matthew 5:21-22, *The Message*)

It would be nice if the childhood idea was true, but reality teaches something else. You've been there. Someone you admired called you an "idiot." Maybe it was an older sibling, or a superior at work, or a "dear" friend. You crawl away broken-hearted. They walk away cocky, unconcerned, unaware.

From Jesus' statement, the words *carelessly* and *thoughtlessly* are vital to realizing the truth in this "simple moral fact." When words are spoken *carelessly*, it is apparent that their impact on the hearer is not important. When words are spewed *thoughtlessly*, whether they build up or destroy is not a concern. Apparently, the only thing important is that the person speaking is free to "speak their mind." That could be one of the mottos of our age. Too often brothers in Christ proudly boast something: "I say what's on my mind. I don't care who it hurts. That's my right. Besides, they have to love me. I'm their brother." Or, a sister in the Lord may "express her feelings" on a matter with words like: "Well, here's what I think…" You can complete the sentence.

Certainly, there is freedom in Christ. If we are to be free anywhere, surely with brothers and sister in Christ is the place. However, does that empower us to spit out words with no regard for who is listening, and how it may affect them – carelessly and thoughtlessly? According to Jesus it does not. Here are a few deadly examples.

You are in a Sunday morning Bible Class that is known for open and lively discussions. You seize the opportunity to "express" your judgments involving the "questionable" actions of an individual. What you did not realize is that a member of that family was in the audience. They left the class wondering why they bothered to come. You left the class feeling refreshed that you had an opportunity to get something off your chest, and commenting on the good discussion. Was it?

You've had dinner with several friends followed by a delicious dessert and coffee. The mood is relaxed. The conversation is light. You share something about your wife while she is in the other room. You preface it with, "This is a great story!" You tell it. Everyone laughs. Then she walks into the room. The laughter stops. She has no idea what you said, but she knows that it hurt. You shyly explain, "It was just a joke. No harm done." Was there?

Your three-year old is having his usual good time walking from the hospital to the parking lot along a long sidewalk. He's not nearly as serious as you think he should be, plus he is a little loud. You scold him using words you would expect him not to use. You think nothing of it. You talk to him that way all the time. He's used to it. Is he?

People look up to you. They know you are a Christian. You've talked about how involved you are with your church. They respect that about you. Then one day something goes wrong. You get upset. You let the words fly. You rant and rave. Your face turns beet red. Your language is anything but godly. But you don't care! You have a right to express yourself. After all, somebody messed up. You justify it by reminding those who hear you that is not healthy to hold that stuff inside. They'll get over it. Will they?

As children, we hope that "words will never hurt" us, but we soon learn otherwise. They can hurt. They do hurt. They cut deeply. The simple moral fact is that words kill. Be careful with your words.

Make your words enjoyable.

We Need to Talk

If I could give a gift to the whole world, every human being that lives and breathes, it would be the ability to communicate. I do not mean to sound as if I have all the answers of how to or how not to communicate, nor do I want to leave the impression that I have the ability to communicate perfectly in any and all situations. That is the reason I began with the word *if*. *If* I could, I would.

Hardly a day passes without a situation that could have been improved, altered, corrected, or eliminated had there been more effective communication. No group seems to be immune to the effects of poor communication. Husbands have a difficult time communicating with their wives. Wives have a difficult time communicating with their husbands (of course, that is because the husbands are such poor communicators). Parents and children have a difficult time communicating. Business associates have difficulty communicating. Determining who is the best communicator is a major part of our current presidential campaign.

The only people who seem to have perfect communication are expectant parents. They seem to be able to perfectly communicate with their yet-to-be-born offspring and this yet-to-be-seen individual communicates perfectly back to the parent. But once they come out of the womb it all changes. Are they hungry or wet? Are they tired or sick? Are they really that obnoxious, or is it just their hormones that have kicked in? How do we communicate with this person? If we assume one thing, it is likely something else. If we try to ignore it, we can't.

Back to my dream gift: If I could give everyone in the world one gift it would be the ability to communicate effectively. Of course, the greatest gift ever given and the most perfect communication was God sending His One Son to the earth to express His love for us. Even with that perfect communication, God's love for man was misunderstood by many. Some thought He was an imposter. Some thought He was coming to take control of the world powers. Some missed Him all together because they were expecting a more dignified king. A Savior that looked like them was not what they were expecting…or wanting.

Regardless of how much I wish I could give this elusive ability to the world, I know I can't. I find I am even having trouble communicating with you about how I wish we could communicate more clearly.

Since I cannot give you the gift, I will make a request: Let's all try harder to give this gift to one another. Husbands, try harder to communicate with your wives, and wives, try harder to communicate with your husbands. Parent, try harder to communicate with your children, and children, try harder to communicate with your parents. Church leaders, try harder to communicate with your flock. Flock, try harder to communicate with your shepherds. Workers, try harder to communicate with your co-workers. Friends, try harder to communicate with your friends. We can try harder.

Although we are the most technologically advanced people in the history of the planet, and we have every gadget imaginable to assist us in being better communicators, we still have a difficult time communicating what is in our heart to the people who are dearest to us. Have we missed something? When God wanted to share His love with us, He sent His son to be with us. Before we invest in more software, or a new computer system, or before we discard the tools we have, perhaps we should simply turn to the people closest to us and share what's in our hearts.

Let's try harder to communicate this week.

Smiling Through Tears

Years ago our family gathered for what had become an all too common time of visitation at the funeral home. In the midst of the words of consolation and regret, someone said something funny. At least it struck us as funny. We all laughed. I mean we really laughed. Not just a quiet snicker or chuckle. We laughed hard. Some may have thought us to be disrespectful or even irreverent, but still we laughed. It felt good. We had cried earlier. We would cry again later. But for those few moments we laughed.

A little girl and her dad were playing and things got a little too rough. She accidentally got hurt and took it personally. Her feelings were hurt. She cried. She got angry. She stuck out her bottom lip. Her dad apologized and dried her tears, but she held on to her pouting disposition. He nudged her a little. She grunted and nudged him back. He did it again. She grunted and nudged him back, but then she smiled through the tears.

A relationship that had shown great promise had ended. His heart was broken. He went home and wept. He vowed never to love again. Then the next week a girl he had seen but never really noticed walked into the classroom. Their eyes met. His heart raced. He smiled.

It had been a long and difficult illness. There had been months of excruciating pain, countless visits to the doctor, examinations, injections, and explanations. With the family surrounding his bed, his final words were spoken, a prayer was worded, and tears flowed. He looked in to each person's eyes, took a last deep breath, and smiled.

She had been in labor all night and most of the day. She was exhausted. He was tired too, but decided it best not to mention it. He was afraid to touch her. She was glad he was afraid to touch her. The progress was slow. They were scared. The nurses reassured them, but they were still concerned. He gripped her hand as the doctor said, "One more good push." They heard the cry. They cried. They kissed. They smiled.

Smiling through tears might be a good description of the life of a

44

disciple of Jesus. We walk through this world with our hand in His, always knowing that graves will be emptied, relationships do survive, broken-hearts can be healed, death is not the end, and pain often precedes the greatest periods of joy. For the person who has sold out to Jesus, even in the darkest of night he knows there will be light in the morning, even in the saddest of times she knows that joy will return, even in the most tragic of deaths they realize there is life yet to be lived, and even in the most despairing of times we understand that hope can sustain us. Why? Because as He hung on the cross and endured its pain, He knew He would rise from the grave. Surely, He smiled through their tears.

He is alive and we can smile through tears.

A Gray Day

The title has nothing to do with the weather. It is a beautiful day. But it is a gray day when it comes to the portrayal of right and wrong. The lines between good and evil, if visible at all, have almost faded from view.

High profile political leaders have crossed the moral line, ignored the boundaries, and manipulated the legal system. When questioned about their behavior they have denied, lied, and skirted the issues.

Teenagers walk in to their schools and open fire on fellow students and teachers. Why? Because they felt left out, were picked on, or just wanted a thrill.

The names of well-known professional athletes are connected to scandal, corruption, and questionable activity. Defending their actions and blaming their critics, they use vulgarities and expletives as they justify their huge salaries, demand their privacy, and praise the Lord in the same breath.

With regularity, television programs portray adultery, homosexuality, and all forms of immorality as the norm. Sponsors of such programs describe their product as enlightening, open-minded, and true to life.

Rock superstars dress scantily, dance provocatively, sing of sensual behavior, and talk of their deep spiritual convictions. All is done in the realm of entertainment.

With such powerful forces at work shaping our minds and influencing our thinking, it is no wonder that our children are confused and adults are bewildered. Where can one go for stability and consistency? Does anyone have any clarification on what is right and wrong?

The answer is a definite yes. God's word contains the guidelines. God's people provide the example. Though they are far from perfect, all over the world there are people who are striving to live according to God's laws. People committed to leaving behind a positive and consistent role model. Young people. Older people. Married people. Single people. Rich people. Poor people. Teachers. Neighbors. Relatives. Each one empowered to live the life of holiness and purity as outlined in Scripture. All reminding us that lies are still lies, murder is still murder, stealing is still stealing.

Are you having a gray day? Confused about how to live your life? Having difficulty remembering what is right and wrong? Turn to His word. Follow one of His children. The day will get clearer.

Enjoy His Way.

It Comes Down to One

There is something about big assemblies that impress us. We watch church attendance to see how big the crowd is. We keep stats on attendance at sporting events, and we are impressed when an attendance record is set. We keep records of all kinds of assemblies as if bigness was the goal. But no matter how big the crowd, it almost always comes down to one.

I recently attended what was said to be the largest assembly of Christian counselors ever held in America. From all over the world, counselors of all shapes, faiths, and sizes assembled to hear and to learn. It was a wonderful experience. Knowledge, wisdom, and skill were abundant. However, the real value in the conference comes down to one: what I do with the information I have received.

Earlier this year several teens and adults from our church participated in what was described as the largest group of Church of Christ teenagers ever assembled. We sang. We studied. We listened. We shared. Then we left. What it boils down to is what each individual teenager and adult does with what we received. It comes down to one.

A few years ago I joined with nearly a million (maybe more) men on the mall of the nation's capital to demonstrate our commitment to be men of God. (If you were there, you may have seen me? I had on blue jeans and was with some other guys.) At one point I thought, "This is too crowded. I'm ready to leave." We heard powerful speakers challenge us to allow God to take control of our lives. When we returned to our homes, our families, and our work place, we realized that while being together is good, it eventually comes down to one question: Will I be a better person?

Every week many of us assemble in churches to worship our God. We hear messages reminding us of what God has in store for us, and where He wants to lead us. We are encouraged when the crowd we have this week is larger than the crowd we had last week. But what really matters is the impact it has on me. Am I different from who I was last week? Is God bigger to me than He was last week?

I am not being critical of the events. Each of the gatherings I have attended were times of great encouragement. There is some value in knowing that there are so many people in the world serious (at least serious enough to attend a big gathering) about serving God. But the value in any event is not the size, the cost, or the attention that event receives. It almost always comes down to one thing: How have I grown?

The Scriptures are filled with stories of men and women who devoted themselves to God, made tremendous sacrifices, and some who gave their lives for His Kingdom. Our history also contains many examples of courageous men and women who have accomplished great things. We need those stories. We need those examples. But more than simply learning the stories, we need to become one of those people. It almost always comes down to one.

Be the one.

Through a Child's Eyes

In the previous three days I had walked through the hotel and convention center at least a dozen times going to and from the conference sessions. Usually intent on not being late and not spilling my coffee, I took little time to notice the sights. When my wife, my daughter, and one of her friends joined me for the last night of the conference quick walks through the hotel came to an end.

As I strolled along with the two children, I saw things I had missed in the previous walks. I knew there was a waterfall, but I had not really looked at the waterfall. I had seen the fountains, but I had not noticed there was a flame of fire in the fountain. Earlier I had walked down the path, but I did not really care where it went. The elevated walkway had been nothing more than a shortcut when I had traveled it earlier. Everything took on a new look as I gazed through the eyes of the children.

Having my eyes opened by my daughter and her friend has prompted me to consider what other interesting things I might be missing.

The ocean seen through the eyes of a child is probably much bigger and more amazing than through these eyes that have out-grown some of their ability to be impressed.

Mountains are not nearly as big through my tired eyes as they were when my eyes were clearer.

A walk through the forest takes much longer if you are walking with a child than if you are walking alone.

A visit to the mall can become an adventure of a lifetime if you are holding the hand of a child.

Perhaps these are some of the reasons Jesus insisted that we *become like little children* (Matthew 18:3) before we enter the Kingdom. His Kingdom looks entirely different when we see it as a child: innocent, trusting, hopeful, joyful.

I'm glad my family joined me for the last night of the conference. I would have missed so much. I pray that I can learn to see more like a child, whether I am walking through a hotel or walking through life. More trusting. More hopeful. More innocent. More dependent. Less suspicious. Less hurried. Seeing things through a child's eyes was the plan from the beginning.

Take time to see the world through a child's eyes.

Lord, What Do You Want from Me?

Have you ever wondered what God wanted you to do with your life? Have you ever wondered if you were doing what He wanted you to do? Have you ever wanted to know that you were doing God's will? Have you ever tried to determine what God's will is for your life? Have you ever felt that no matter what you did it was not enough?

If you answered "No" to all these questions, then you can stop reading. I have nothing to offer you. However, if you answered "Yes" to any of these questions, then maybe you will find something worth reading.

In Micah 6 the Lord is calling His people to be accountable for their actions. They have rebelled against God. Israel has been found guilty, and apparently, they are about to experience God's wrath. Like anyone who has been found guilty, they want to know what they can do to avoid punishment and to make things right. They want to know what is good in God's eyes.

Their tendency is to go before God *with burnt offerings...with thousands of rams* (Micah 6:6,7). In our day, we might try: "Should I write a bigger check?" "Should I come to church more regularly?" "Would You like for me to sing louder and more spirited?" "Would reading my Bible every day be sufficient?"

The Lord has a different idea: *He has showed you, O man, what is good. And what does the Lord require of you? To act justly and to love mercy and to walk humbly with your God.* – Micah 6:8

To act justly may not be the popular thing to do. We are hearing a lot about justice right now. Some like it. Some do not. God does. This is what He wants. This is what He requires. This is His will.

To love mercy means more than simply being a mercy-lover. To really love mercy involves a willingness to work toward showing mercy. It involves a demonstration of God's mercy to those who need it. Those we like. Those we love. Those we know. Even those we may not like, love or know very well. God wants this. God requires this. This is His will.

To *walk humbly with your God* indicates that we understand our relationship with Him. We know that He is in charge. I envision a child walking hand in hand with his or her daddy. Trusting Him completely. Innocently. Submissively. This is His will. God wants this. God requires this.

I don't presume that these three statements will be all you need to understand God's will for every detail of your life. But maybe it is a start. Maybe if we focused more on these, the others would fall into place.

Lord, what do You want from me? *To act justly, to love mercy and to walk humbly with your God.*

Are you willing?

SLOW DOWN!

The message on the flashing sign on the side of the freeway naturally caught my attention: SLOW DOWN! I did. When I read those words, I interpreted them as more than a command from the law enforcement officers. For some reason, I sensed a pleading in those words: PLEASE SLOW DOWN! Perhaps that was the intent. Perhaps that was the message of my heart pleading with me: Tom, please slow down.

You see I noticed that sign as I raced from one part of town to another in an effort to get some Christmas shopping done. Time is running out, you know. Not many shopping days left. All the good deals are going to be gone if I don't hurry. So, I was hurrying. In fact, all day long I had been hurrying. I had hurried to get my daughter to school. I had hurried through an early morning stop at the local Walmart. I had hurried to get to the coffee shop so I could hurriedly enjoy a cup of coffee and a bagel while I hurriedly read a couple of chapters in a book about fathers and daughters which, in part, is telling me not to hurry in that relationship. I hurried to the "Y" so I could get my workout done, so I could hurry to get more shopping done, so I could hurry back to the house where I hoped to have some time when I didn't have to hurry. That's when I saw the sign. SLOW DOWN!

As I try to follow the advice of the sign on the side of the road I want to plead with you as well: PLEASE SLOW DOWN!

Slow down and enjoy the Christmas season. Have you read the story yet this season? Slow down and read it. As you read, look for the times hurrying is mentioned in the story. Do you read anything about the Savior being in a hurry? Does it say that the shepherds were rushing their flock, or were they watching their flock? Do you read that it says Mary was tired of carrying the baby Jesus and ready to get it over with? Do you read about the angels speeding through the delivery of their message, "Peace on earth and good will to men?" No matter how hard I try, or how fast I read, my Bible doesn't read that way.

So, I plead with you to slow down. Slow down long enough to enjoy buying the gifts, instead of being one of those shoppers who rush home with their treasures so they can say they have something under the tree. I plead with you to slow down and enjoy the gatherings with your friends. I plead with you to slow down during the meals so you can enjoy the delicious foods that have been so carefully prepared. I plead with you to slow down and enjoy this season when giving really is more important than getting. I plead with you to slow down so you do not miss the message that in this season, and in every season, "God is with us."

PLEASE SLOW DOWN! Relax. Take a break. Enjoy. Remember: "'Tis the season to be jolly."

Try to slow down.

Be Nice

As the assistant coach for my daughter's basketball team, my job is to help the head coach teach the girls some of the fundamentals of the game. Dribbling. Passing. Defense. Shooting. Playing as a team. Most of the coaching in this instructional league really takes place in the thirty minutes of practice prior to the game. Once the ball is tipped it is difficult, at best, to get ten, eleven, and twelve-year-old girls to understand the value of setting a good screen, or to grasp the importance of blocking-out in order to get a rebound.

At this age, the aggressive "we-gotta-win" mentality has not yet taken over. Their innocence is still very evident at this stage of the game. In one game a girl bumped into another while they both were going after a loose ball. She stopped and said, "Oh, I'm sorry." Another time I heard one of the girls say, "Excuse me," as she tried to take the ball away from one of the girls on the other team. Last week as a substitution was made, one of the girls on the opposing teams yelled back at the bench: "I don't know who I'm guarding." From our bench one of our girls said, "You were guarding me, now you're guarding…" I reminded her that in a real game you might not want to do that. (After all, it is an instructional league.)

She gave me a puzzled look, and I wished I had not said anything. Even now as I reflect on the incident, I wish I had kept my instructions to myself. I wish I had said instead, "That was a nice thing to do. Don't ever stop being nice."

When we wonder what has happened to all the nice people, perhaps we should look to a basketball court full of little girls. Maybe we should think about how we may actually be teaching our kids not to be so nice. Do we really want them to learn not to be nice? Maybe we should ask ourselves if the high cost of winning at any cost is really worth the cost.

I am reminded of a statement that my daughter has somewhat adopted as one of her favorites: "It's nice to be important, but it's more important to be nice." We would do well not to work so hard to teach our children not to be so nice. I am glad this is an instructional league. I think I may be learning something.

Be nice.

Only Slightly Off

The kids had the day off from school so my daughter, one of her friends, and I were having lunch. I enjoyed their laughter. We talked about the food, boys, and life in general. I had noticed a strange phone number on my cell phone, and we discussed who it might have been. After some discussion, my daughter's friend made an interesting statement: "Have you ever noticed how in a phone number if you get one number wrong, the whole thing is wrong?" My daughter and I joked about her statement, yet we came to realize as we thought about it that there was a profoundness in her statement.

For instance, in some situations one mistake does not mean total failure. If you a taking a test and you miss one problem, you have not blown the entire test. Just one problem. If you are in a basketball game and miss one shot, chances are you have not lost the whole game. If you are playing golf and mess up on one hole you always have the next hole. If you are playing the piano and miss one note you have not ruined the entire piece of music. Being slightly off does not always mean disaster. There is room for error in some situations.

However, in other areas, as in telephone numbers, there is no room for error. If you are addressing a letter, one number can delay the delivery. If you are counting money, one misplaced decimal can make a major difference. If you are keeping score in a ball game, one wrong score can mean the difference between a win and a loss. If you are looking for an address, one number can make the difference between finding whom you are looking for and meeting a total stranger. If you are programming your VCR one wrong number can mean the difference between seeing what you planned to see and being very frustrated. One letter omitted in an email address means the message will not get to the intended recipient. Being slightly off does sometimes make a difference.

My young friend is not only right about how being slightly off can make a difference in phone numbers, but being slightly off can have even greater ramifications when it involves how we live life. Jesus said, *"Not everyone who calls me 'Lord, Lord,' will enter the kingdom of heaven, but only he who does the will of my Father who is in heaven"* (Matthew 7:21). One might think that just saying the words would be enough, but Jesus says otherwise. The rich young ruler was right about most of his life, but he was lacking one thing. That was enough to change eternity. In Matthew 25, we have a scene where it appears that many people had lived fairly decent lives, but they missed out when it came to really centering in on what mattered. There are some things where being slightly off makes a major difference.

I'm glad that we have a Father who forgives innocent mistakes and overlooks some of our foolish errors. But He cannot and will not overlook it when we fail to live the life He wants us to live. In that case, being slightly off is very costly. This slight error in judgement can mean the difference between eternity with God and eternity separated from God. Just saying the words is not enough. There must be a life that is consistent with the words.

If you dial a wrong number, chances are all you need to do is say, "Excuse me." If you fail to live the life, you could miss it all.

Live the life.

Cutting Corners

One of the places I like to jog is a trail behind a church not far from our home. The trail is a peaceful place with trees along three sides and a playground on the fourth. Inside the track is a ball field and a lush green field guarded by "Please Keep Off the Grass" signs. There is seldom anyone else on the track when I'm there which allows me to make my five or six laps without bothering, or being bothered, by anyone.

One day while making the first turn I noticed that the actual gravel covered trail makes a pretty sharp, almost ninety-degree turn to the left. Apparently, like myself, several others have literally rounded the corner. To save three or four steps (which can be a lot when you feel like you cannot take one more step), walkers and runners have cut the corner so often that the alternative route looks like it is as popular as the real trail. As I found myself cutting the corner on every lap I began to think there are times when I'm glad we can cut corners and times when I'm glad we don't cut corners. (If you jog, you understand why I think about things like this.)

I'm glad I can cut the corner when I'm late for an appointment. I'm glad I can cut the corner on certain golf holes. I'm glad when I can cut corners in finishing a project. Sometimes cutting corners is a good thing

There are other times when cutting corners is not such a good idea. If you are playing golf and cutting the corner means going over the trees, and you are not sure you can get over the trees, don't cut the corner. If you are cooking a meal and run out of an important ingredient, please don't cut corners. If you are my dentist and think you can drill a little deeper without deadening the nerve, please don't cut the corner. If you are my doctor and see something on an x-ray but decide you can cut a corner to save me time and money, I'm not so sure I want you to cut corners. If you are building my house, please don't cut too many corners unless it saves me a whole lot of money and will make me very happy.

Spiritually there are not many situations in which you will want to cut corners. Don't cut corners when it comes to loving God. He said, *"Love me with your all your heart, soul, mind and strength"* (Mark 12:30). Don't be cutting corners when it comes to prayer. He said, *"Pray without ceasing"* (1 Thessalonians 5:17). Don't cut corners when it comes to sharing the Good News. He said, *"Go into all the world and make disciples"* (Matthew 28:19). Don't cut corners when it comes to your relationship with the Lord. He said, *"Whoever wants to be my disciple must deny himself, take up his cross and follow me"* (Matthew 16:24).

When you're jogging and find a corner that will save you a few steps, it is probably all right to cut the corner. When it comes to your spiritual life, you will do well to stay on the main path.

Be careful of cutting corners.

Being Used by God

He has made major mistakes in his life. Some of those mistakes have produced serious pain and sorrow in those who love him. At one point, he did not know if his life was worth living. He was on the verge of destruction. He surrendered his life to God. Now he has purpose and direction. He has experienced God's grace and is actively sharing a message of hope. He is being used by God.

She has taught elementary school for over twenty years. When she gets home she sometimes forgets to stop using her teacher voice when she speaks to her husband and her own children. There are times she wonders if she is making a difference. One day a little boy came up to her desk after school and told her his mother was very sick. She put down her pen and papers and held him in her arms. She is being used by God.

He works for a major corporation. Most days he feels fairly insignificant and unappreciated. One day he noticed a coworker seemed low-spirited so he invited him to lunch. He listened to the story of a broken home, a broken heart, and shattered dreams. He offered a few words of comfort, but mostly he listened. He is being used by God.

She is young and inexperienced in the ways of ministry, but she loves the Lord. She wants to make a difference. She spent the summer in a strange town, living with a strange family, meeting new people, making new friends, teaching God's Word, and demonstrating the Godly life. She made a difference. She is being used by God.

He is getting older. His health is failing. He cannot do all that he once did. He welcomes visitors. He gives a friendly smile. He encourages. He prays. He uses his gifts for the Lord. He wants to do more. He is being used by God.

She doesn't drive at night, and there are some days when her arthritis makes it difficult to move. But she prays for her family, her friends, and her church. She often sends cards of encouragement and notes that are timely and sweet. She is being used by God.

He is not old enough to drive. He is not yet into dating. He's a teenager and trying to find his way with the Lord. There are times when he is confused and frustrated with life. He traveled to a foreign country to help those who needed his help. He is being used by God.

He is a young man with lots of potential. He is searching to find his place in the world. There are times when he struggles with the difference between what could be and what is. He tries to keep his hopes alive. During the summer, he has invested himself in the lives of young children. They look up to him. They admire him. He has changed them by his presence in their lives. He is being used by God.

God may never call us to preach to the masses. He may never lead us to a foreign mission field. But He will work in us and through us to minister to those in need. He will use us if we will allow ourselves to be used by Him.

I tell you the truth, anyone who gives a cup of cold water in my name because you belong to Christ will certainly not lose his reward. – Mark 9:41

Let Him use you.

Starting Over...Again

Dear Father, I have spoken these words before, but now I am speaking them again. I have failed you...again. I have not lived up to my commitment. Please forgive me. I want to start over...again.

Have you ever prayed a prayer like that before? You know the promises you have made. You know the promises you have failed to keep. You know the feelings of failure. You know the feelings of guilt. You know the regrets. You know what it feels like to want to start over...again.

You lost your temper again. There you were in front of all those kids. You're the adult. You're the coach. You're supposed to be a good example. You said you'd never do that again. But you did. Now you feel awful. You're starting over...again.

You had said you would never act like that again. You had embarrassed yourself before and were determined not to let it happen ever again. You were at a party. You took one drink. Then another. Then another. And another. You do not remember what happened after that, but from the looks you received when you walked into the office on Monday morning it must have been pretty bad. Now, you are starting over...again.

You knew the relationship was not healthy, and you had avoided him for several weeks. You had said it was over. When he offered you a ride home, you thought you were in control. One thing led to another, and before you knew it you were walking into your house crying and consumed by guilt. Once more you are telling yourself that you are starting over...again.

When you were baptized, you thought all your sinning days were behind you. You were cruising along really well, then those old habits began to creep back into your life. Your conversation included words you had vowed never to speak. You began to laugh at jokes you once thought were crude and inappropriate. Your involvement in spiritual activities became less and less. You realize that it is time to be starting over...again.

Throughout history God's people have proven that there are times when we start over, and there are times when we must start over...again. In a statement we typically use in reference to entire nations, God has given us all a promise of what He will do when we are committed to starting over...again. *If my people, who are called by my name, will humble themselves and pray and seek my face and turn from their wicked ways, then I will hear from heaven and will forgive their sin and will heal their land.* – 2 Chronicles 7:14

The instructions are simple: Call on His name. Humble yourself. Pray and seek His face. Turn from your wicked ways. He will hear and forgive and heal. Again and again. If you are in need of starting over again, you can be certain that He is listening to your call for help. He is willing to forgive you. He will heal you.

Let Him help...again.

Pushing Too Many Buttons

As I backed out of the garage I reached to press the button to close the garage door. I pushed the button to close the sunroof on my car at the same time. While my hand was up above my head I decided to also try to push the button on the clip that holds my sunglasses on the visor. Simple routine actions, right? Simple when you do them one at a time, but when you try to push them all at the same time while backing out of the garage and holding a cup of coffee, it is not so simple. Add to this little morning scenario the fact that I was distracted with the events of the day before and the plans for the day ahead. So, what happened is that the sunroof only closed half way (you must keep the button pressed or it automatically stops at the halfway point). Forgetting that I had already pressed the garage door opener (closer) button, I pushed it again. The door stopped. I pushed it again and it went back up. So, I pushed it again to close it while holding down the sunroof button. In the meantime, the button on the clip that holds my sunglasses in place released my sunglasses which had now fallen on the floor beneath my feet. (No, I did not try to retrieve them…immediately that is.)

At this point, near the end of my driveway, I sensed that this was not a good start to the day so I stopped, took a deep breath, made sure all the buttons were pressed properly (including the button to change the radio station), retrieved my sunglasses, took another deep breath, mentally said a prayer, and proceeded on my way.

Some readers may be thinking, "This guy needs help! Who gets stressed out over trying to close his garage door?" The answer to that question is anybody who is also trying to press every other button in sight at the same time. Maybe it is not a garage door opener button, or a sunroof button that is getting you stressed. But you see all the buttons in your life that need to be pushed, and you are trying to push them all at the same time.

You are a wife, a mother, a daughter, a sister, an employee, a coworker, a church member, a friend, and a follower of Jesus. Each of these roles comes attached to a specific set of responsibilities and privileges. Each one representing a button that demands to be pushed. Right now!

You are a husband, a father, a son, a brother, an employee, a coworker, a friend, and a follower of Jesus. Not only are you aware of the responsibilities of those roles, but you also consider it a privilege and want to push all those buttons. Right now!

You are a student, a son (or daughter), you work as much as you can, you are trying to make good grades to keep your scholarship (or get a scholarship), you are trying to build a relationship that will last, and at the same time maintain other relationships that have already lasted a long time. Each one is a button waiting to be pushed.

Now you find yourself backing out of your driveway trying to close the garage, trying to close the sunroof, trying to change the radio station, and fiddling with the thing on the visor that holds your sunglasses all at the same time. What you realize is that none of them are actually getting the attention they need.

How do you do it? How are you supposed to do it? Is it possible to do it? Is it essential that you do it? Should you try to push all the buttons right now?

Here's a suggestion: Stop! Take a long deep breath. Look at what you are doing and how you are living. Is it really necessary to push all those buttons at the same time? Are there some that can be pushed later, or not at all? Determine which one absolutely must be pushed right now. Push it. Then take another deep breath and push another one. Or not. Make sure that every button you pushed is pushed with all your desire and skill. Give it your complete attention.

Jesus once said, *"Be careful, or your hearts will be weighed down with dissipation, drunkenness and the anxieties of life, and the day will close on you unexpectedly like a trap."* (Luke 21:34) You may not be struggling with the "dissipation and drunkenness" but the "anxieties of life" may be choking the life right out of your soul. All the buttons are demanding to be pushed at one time.

Oh, one final suggestion. If you find yourself trying to do all those things as you back out of your driveway, and it happens to be raining, don't worry about the garage door, the radio, or the sunglasses clip…close the sunroof first. Sometimes the priority is obvious.

Push one button at a time.

Not from a Worldly Point of View

This passage has been bouncing around in my head for quite some time: *So from now on we regard no one from a worldly point of view. Though we once regarded Christ in this way, we do so no longer. Therefore, if anyone is in Christ, he is a new creation; the old has gone, the new has come!* – 2 Corinthians 5:16,17

I believe Landon Saunders first introduced me to the thought that how I treat a person is greatly influenced by how I view them. The challenge for me is this: I will no longer regard anyone from a worldly point of view.

If I no longer regard a person from a worldly point of view, when I look at the guy behind the cash register at the convenience store, maybe I will see him differently. Instead of only seeing the seven piercings in his ear, lip, nose, and cheek (there were more but I could not count them all without being really rude), I will look at him. A real human being created in the image of the Creator.

If I no longer regard a person from a worldly point of view, when I walk through the intensive care unit of the hospital, maybe I will see more than the tubes and the machines. Maybe I will see one of God's children on the verge of the threshold of eternity. Maybe I will not be in a hurry to leave.

If I no longer regard a person from a worldly point of view, maybe I will really see my children. Maybe I will look at them like God looks at them. Maybe I will see them, not just their actions. Maybe I will listen to their heart, not just their attitude. Maybe I will be more careful with how my words affect them. Maybe I will be more concerned about how I spend my time with them.

If I no longer regard a person from a worldly point of view, maybe I will be slower to speak, and quicker to listen. Maybe I will speak more gently. Maybe I will spend more time with people. Maybe I will be more concerned about what they are getting out of our visit and less concerned about what I am getting.

69

If I no longer regard a person from a worldly point of view, when I look at a person, maybe I will really look *at* them and not past them. When I listen to them, maybe I will really listen to what they are saying and not simply wait for them to get quiet so I can speak.

If I no longer regard a person from a worldly point of view, maybe I will see my wife as the gift God has given me to love, honor, and cherish. Maybe I will appreciate her more. Maybe I will seek to please her and not be angry when she does not please me.

If I no longer regard a person from a worldly point of view, maybe when I see someone hurting, crying, alone, or in need, I will seek to relieve their pain, dry their tear, spend time with them, and fill their need. Maybe I will be less selfish. Maybe I will be more thoughtful. Maybe I will be more forgiving. Maybe I will be more accepting. Maybe I will respond to them with more tenderness.

If I no longer regard a person from a worldly point of view, not only will I see that person in a different light, maybe they will see me in a different light. Maybe, just maybe, they will begin to see me as the "new creation" that I am. Maybe they will see that the "old has gone, the new has come."

Maybe...

Doing What You Think is Right

As the Coalition Forces carry out their mission in Iraq, hundreds of thousands of others throughout the world have taken to the streets with either signs of protest or signs of support. Some call it just. Some call it unjust. Some say it is what needs to be done. Some say it is illegal and exemplifies imperialism. I have no grand notion of these few words in this limited space bringing about a significant change in anyone's point of conviction. However, I do hope to shed some meaningful light on the idea of doing what we think is right.

Let me acknowledge in the outset, I do realize that one can do what he thinks is right and be totally wrong. I have done that many times. You have, too. Doing what we think is right is something that has been implanted in our brains by our parents, who have had it impressed upon them by their parents, and something we consistently teach our own children. One of the primary goals of any God-fearing parent is to teach their children to learn to do what is right no matter who or how many others are doing something else. If we have given them God's Word as a guide, we must release them into the world with a prayer for guidance by the Spirit that they will make wise choices and do what is right.

Doing what we think is right carries obvious consequences. If I do what I think is right, I will often find myself standing alone. Jesus talked about the "narrow gate" as the way of His leading. Standing alone does not guarantee one is right, but when one does what he thinks is right, he can almost always expect to stand alone.

If I do what I think is right some will consider me arrogant. There is little that can be done to convince them otherwise. If someone thinks I am arrogant because I have chosen to do what I think is right (and I am certain that my motives are pure and based on my understanding of God's leadership in my life), there can be only two options: I can give in to the pressure to conform, or I can do what I think is right and be considered arrogant.

No doubt many great men and women have taken a stand for what they believed to be right and received considerable criticism. Abraham Lincoln may have been called arrogant a time or two for his stand against slavery. There were probably times he felt he was standing alone. He did what he thought was right. Moses did what he thought was right by following God's leadership instead of listening to the wishes of the people. Do you suppose anyone ever voiced a complaint against Moses along the lines, "Who does he think he is? You'd think God had spoken directly to him or something?" He did what he thought was right. As Jesus moved in the direction of Calvary, some who opposed Him said, "He claims to be the Son of God!" Some who believed in Him rebuked Him and told Him that they had a better way. He did what He thought was right.

Every mother and father who have ever made an unpopular decision for their family have had to settle matters in their own minds and do what they thought was right. Every wife who has ever decided either to go along with her husband or to suggest another plan has had to do what she thought was right. Every child has or will face countless decisions that will come down to one question: What do you think is right? After seeking God's wisdom through prayer and the study of His Word (not conscience or popular opinion), the best any of us can do is do what we think is right. That is all any of us should expect from each other.

It is easy right now to sit in our homes with the remote control in our hand and profess to know what is right and what is wrong. It is easy to criticize, judge, and second guess those who are leading our nation and are leading us into battle. That is our right. We are free to play armchair president, armchair general, and armchair peace activist. Because of who we are and where we live, we have that right to criticize, judge, and second guess. But as we make that choice to do what we think is right, we must remember that those who are leading us are also doing what they think is right. There is room for both.

Is the President right in his decision to send U. S. troops into Iraq? I don't know. He believes he is. Are those marching for peace right? I don't know. They believe they are. Are the leaders of your church right in their decisions as they shepherd the flock? I don't know. They believe they are. Are the parents right in the decisions they make? I don't know. They believe they are. Are the children right in the decisions they make? I don't know. They believe they are.

I just hope we will try to make room for all of us as we try to do what we think is right.

I Didn't Realize I was Moving

I stepped into the hotel elevator and pushed the button for my desired floor. As I waited, I wondered to myself, "When is this thing going to start moving." Suddenly the door opened and I realized I had moved several flights down without even knowing it. There was no sound to indicate I was moving. There was no jolt to indicate I had started moving. And there was no bump at the end to indicate I had been moving. I didn't realize I was moving. I've noticed the same thing to be true in other areas of life.

There was a day when most television programs were family based and for the most part wholesome. Other than my regular Saturday night ritual of trying to out-draw Marshall Matt Dillon at the beginning of *Gunsmoke*, I rarely saw killing. Miss Kitty was apparently the Marshall's girlfriend, but if anything inappropriate ever happened, no one ever knew it. (It was not until many years later that I understood what Miss Kitty did for a living.) I did not realize that we had moved, but things have changed. Many of the regulars in prime-time programming today make no pretense of the lead characters' lack of morality. More often than not the lack of morals is praised and glorified. We were moving, but we are only now beginning to realize how fast and far we were moving.

There was a day when professional athletes and coaches felt an obligation to their fans to be men and women of integrity…at least publicly. If they were guilty of adultery, drunkenness, or any form of immorality, they would have tried to keep their deeds of darkness in the dark. No longer! We now hear boasting about the number of women they have slept with, the amount of alcohol consumed, or the amount of money spent on fast automobiles and huge houses. We've moved, but I'm not sure we realized it…or if we are concerned about it.

There was a day when things were simpler and safer – or so it seemed. We did not lock our doors at night or when we were away from home. There was no need to lock our car doors because there was nothing inside we were concerned about being stolen. Even if we did have something of importance, we would have never considered that anyone would steal it. We did not need metal detectors or police officers in our schools. The number of troublemakers in school were in the minority; the good kids stood up for what was right and were respected for their stand. We have moved from those simple days, but the move has been gradual and we did not seem to notice.

There was a day when one word in *Gone with the Wind* caused a scandal. Now movies are filled with curse words and vulgarity and praised as being "true to life." We now find it acceptable for public figures (politicians, comedians, movie stars, and athletes) to use foul language any time they choose – interviews, during the game, commercials, and talk shows. Such things are often justified by saying they reflect our culture, but I wonder which one is reflecting which. We are moving, but we do not seem to notice.

There was once a man who noticed that his friends were moving in an unhealthy direction. Not only did he notice their movement, he wanted to do something about it. So, he wrote, *It is actually reported that there is sexual immorality among you, and of a kind that does not occur even among pagans: A man has his father's wife. And you are proud! Shouldn't you rather have been filled with grief and have put out of your fellowship the man who did this? Even though I am not physically present, I am with you in spirit. And I have already passed judgment on the one who did this, just as if I were present. When you are assembled in the name of our Lord Jesus and I am with you in spirit, and the power of our Lord Jesus is present, hand this man over to Satan, so that the sinful nature may be destroyed and his spirit saved on the day of the Lord. Your boasting is not good. Don't you know that a little yeast works through the whole batch of dough?* (1 Corinthians 5:1-6). They were moving, but they did not notice.

The elevator in the hotel was so fast and smooth that I moved from floor to floor without noticing. We tend to do the same thing in life. We must be careful that we not drift into areas that are not healthy without realizing. Some move into sinful lifestyles without noticing. Some find themselves stuck in the tentacles of sin without ever noticing they were moving. Be careful of the drift.

Are you aware that you are moving?

Walking in the Shadows

As the U. S. Open reached its conclusion at Olympia Fields Country Club just outside of Chicago last weekend (Father's Day, June 15, 2003) another story was unfolding within the main story. First there was the championship itself. This year's champion was Jim Furyk. He tied the U. S. Open record with an eight under par performance. He became only the third player in U. S. Open history to ever reach double figures. Throughout the day's round, the television commentators spoke often of the close relationship he had with his father who is also the only coach he has ever had. As he accepted his trophy (and the sizable check), he turned his tear-filled eyes away from the camera, toward his dad, and said, "Happy Father's Day." That in itself is a great story. But there is another.

Even before Furyk sank his last putt to win the championship (yes, I did watch the whole thing), another amazing drama was being played out on that same course. This is also a story of victory, but perhaps on an even grander scale. This is the story of Bruce Edwards. Edwards has been Tom Watson's caddie since 1973. He has carried Watson's bag through "the thrill of victory and the agony of defeat" for thirty years. At the end of Thursday's round, Watson thrilled all fans old and young alike by sharing the lead at five under par at the ripe old age of 53. For those who don't follow golf, that's not the norm. But there is more to this story.

Last January, Edwards was diagnosed with lateral sclerosis – Lou Gehrig's disease. There is no known cure. Watson is using his celebrity status to call attention to the disease and has committed to take care of his friend's medical expenses. He spoke not only of the disease in every interview I saw but also emotionally shared his love for his friend. As the week unfolded, more and more people became aware of Edward's condition. On the last day, the crowd began to express their appreciation.

A good two hours before the USGA crowned a new champion, Watson and Edwards received something few would expect in the modern world of sports. As they approached the green on every hole, the appreciative crowd stood, applauded, and chanted, "Bruce! Bruce! Bruce!" As they approached the 18th, Watson and Edwards walked side by side with Watson's hand on Edwards' shoulder and received what may have been the loudest cheers of the day.

For thirty years Bruce Edwards has been unknown. For thirty years he has walked with Tom Watson over thousands of miles of the world's greatest golf courses in all kinds of weather. He has shared the ups and downs that go with any competitive sport. As friends, they have no doubt also shared some of life's most difficult storms. He has encouraged Watson, he has advised him, and he has surely felt the pain and the joy. He has done it quietly and from the shadows. That is role of a caddie. His job is not to take the spotlight. His job is not to receive the applause. His job is to carry the bag, rack the traps, clean the clubs, and encourage his pro. He has done his job well. Maybe on Sunday he received his greatest paycheck.

I've talked about Edwards not to focus on golf (although that's not a bad subject), but to focus on the fact that most of us will never win the U. S. Open, or any open for that matter. Most of us will never stand before millions of viewers and be able to say before the whole world, "Happy Father's Day." Most of us will never be famous. Most of us will never be dubbed the "greatest." But all of us have the opportunity to encourage.

We all, every day, have the opportunity to say an encouraging word, write an encouraging note, give an encouraging hug, or offer a prayer of encouragement. We all, every day, are given someone who needs us to help carry their bag, clean up their mess, or cheer for their success. We do it by fulfilling our role. We do it by filling our place in the Kingdom. We do it by walking in the shadows.

Bruce Edwards has walked in the shadow of Tom Watson for thirty years. Mike Furyk has walked in the shadow of his son. Behind the scenes, unknown to others, they have done their job and done it well. They have received some of their reward. You will, too. Maybe not on national television or with a large paycheck, but your reward is waiting. God has not forgotten you. Your deeds as you walk in the shadows are not unnoticed.

As you walk in the shadows doing God's work, remember you are not forgotten.

Keep walking in the shadows.

Distractions

Distractions come in all shapes and sizes. Distractions have no respect for time or sense of timing. Distractions can be good, but by the very definition, usually are not. Distractions reduce our productivity and increase our level of frustrations. Distractions prevent us from becoming whom we want to become and from doing what we are capable of doing.

Gifted athletes will never reach full potential unless they learn to manage their distractions. Championship teams are champions, in part, because they learn to deal appropriately with distractions. Coaches have a hard time coaching and players have a hard time playing when they are dealing with distractions.

Teachers find it difficult to teach when there are distractions. Students find it difficult to learn when there are distractions.

Parents find it difficult to talk with their children when there are distractions. Children find it hard to feel loved when their parents are distracted. Couples find it hard to work on their relationship because of distractions from children or from their busy schedules.

Readers can't read when they are distracted. Writers find it…difficult…to…write…when there are… (excuse me, I was distracted) distractions.

Distractions are everywhere. We try to read our Bible, but we get distracted. We try to pray, but we get distracted.

As Jesus prepared his disciples for ministry, He faced many distractions: crowds of needy people, stubborn and hardened hearts, worldly thinking from His followers, confusion, misperceptions, and people with their own agenda for Jesus' life. To avoid and escape the distractions, Jesus often went away to quiet places to be alone. There were times when He took His disciples with Him to avoid the distractions.

The New Testament suggests that handling distractions is a battle of the mind: *Set your minds on things above…* – Colossians 3:2; *…think on such things.* – Philippians 4:8; *…fix your eyes on Jesus…* – Hebrews 12:2.

Jesus said it this way, *"Be careful or your hearts will be weighed down with dissipation, drunkenness and the anxieties of life, and that day will come on you unexpectedly like a trap."* (Luke 21:34)

Chances are, if you are still reading this article (and apparently you are), you have been distracted at least once by a child needing your attention, a phone call, another email, your "To Do" list, or a bird singing outside your window. If you have not been distracted, you probably will be before long. I'm not as concerned that you may be distracted while reading this article as I am that you may be distracted from your walk with God.

You may be reading this article in an effort to keep or regain your focus. You may be struggling with distractions. Your eyes are being distracted. Your heart is being distracted. Your attention is being distracted. Satan loves to distract us. Be careful. Keep your focus. Fix your eyes on Jesus.

A Quiet Place

You have heard sermons on it (I've preached sermons on it). You have read about it (I've written about it). You have seen examples of it (I've referred to some of those examples). It has been talked about, written about, prayed about, pondered, considered, suggested, requested, and demanded. No matter how much is written or spoken, there is nothing like meeting God in a quiet place.

Jesus demonstrated the importance of finding a quiet place. Hearing the news of the death of John the Baptist, Jesus *withdrew by boat privately to a solitary place* (Matthew 14:13). He apparently regularly went out early in the morning to a quiet place: *Very early in the morning, while it was still dark, Jesus got up, left the house and went off to a solitary place, where he prayed* (Mark 1:35; Luke 4:42). There were times when He took a few of His disciples away from the crowd to a quiet place: *So they went away by themselves in a boat to a solitary place* (Mark 6:32).

How do you find a quiet place, and what do you do when you get there? Here are a few suggestions.

First, you will need to search for the quiet place. Chances are such a place will not just appear in front of you. You may find a physical place where you can go for some quiet time as you go about your everyday business, but you will not get there unless you are intentional about it. Search for a place and a time where you can be alone with God.

Second, finding a quiet place does not ensure anything of value will happen. There are people who spend thousands of dollars and travel long distances to be in quiet places, but all they accomplish is that they were in a quiet place. It was quiet, but God's presence was not acknowledged. Jesus did more than just go to quiet places.

Third, once you are in a quiet place, be quiet. Turn off the television. Turn off the radio. Turn off the telephone. Turn off your mind. Do your best to not think about all the things the genius of distractions will try to use to make you to lose your focus. Then just be quiet.

Now, if those three suggestions are not enough, here's the real tough one. Listen. Don't talk. Don't read (unless it is the Word). Just listen. Listen to the sounds of nature. Listen to the wind. Listen to your heart. Listen to what God is saying to you. Be quiet and listen.

What can you expect from this experience? You may feel a sense of refreshment. You may be able to discern something of God's will for your life. You may understand yourself better. You may get a handle on what has been troubling you. You may realize that you need more times like this. You may simply enjoy the quiet.

I offer only one guarantee: if you don't learn to find a quiet place to be with God, you will miss God. God will not compete for attention. He will not compete with all the busy details of life. He is concerned about them, knows about them, and longs to hear about them, but He will not compete for them. He will allow us to go as long and as hard as we choose to go and never demand that we stop for Him. Yet, He is always there, ready, willing, and able to refresh our spirit when we make the time.

I am writing this with the hope that something that I have said will encourage you to slow down and find a quiet place with God. Some of you really need it. Some of your children really need you to slow down. The pace some of you are keeping is not healthy—physically, emotionally, or spiritually. I am constantly being reminded that if finding a quiet and solitary place was necessary and beneficial for the Son of God, surely it is necessary and will be beneficial for you and me.

Quiet in His presence.

Gifts That Last

I don't mean to sound like a Scrooge, but most of the gifts that we exchange on Christmas morning will not last. Food will either be eaten or disposed of. Clothing will wear out, go out of style, or be passed down to others. Even the big gifts like new cars (yeah, I dream big), computers, stereos, and super-duper home theater systems will eventually lose their appeal or become outdated. Let's face it: most of the gifts and wrappings will be gone long before we will. Is there anything we can give that will last? There is.

One gift that will last is the love shown to other people. When Jesus prepared to leave His disciples, one of the things He was most concerned about was teaching them to love one another. He went so far as to say, *This is how people will know that you are my disciples. If you love one another* (John 13:35). If it was important to Jesus, it must be important to us. We demonstrate our love for people by the gifts we give and to whom they are given. Do we tend to give gifts to those we know will give us a gift, or from whom we have received a gift? Or do we share with those who have no ability to repay or respond? Give your love to someone.

Another lasting gift is the gift of joy. Remember the message the shepherds heard at the birth of Jesus was, *We bring you good news of great joy* (Luke 2:10). There are people near you who need a huge serving of joy. The widow next door. The man who always sits alone in church. The gentleman who just lost his wife. The couple who lost their baby. The parents whose son is in the war. The single guy who always tries to act cool. The mother and children spending Christmas without her husband and their daddy. There will be presents under the tree, but will those presents really bring joy to the world? Give them your joy.

What about peace? Could you be an instrument of peace in someone's world? Could you be the tool that God has chosen to calm the storm in the life of a co-worker? Or could the child in your class who has been disruptive, unruly, and hard to deal with all year benefit from your peaceful spirit? Share your peace with someone.

Do you known anyone who would be surprised to be the recipient of your patience this Christmas? We could all probably use a little kindness, couldn't we? How about goodness? Is there a friend who has been betrayed? Perhaps they would appreciate your faithfulness. The whole world could use more gentleness. Do you suppose there is someone who would appreciate your self-control?

These gifts won't fit under your tree very well, and they don't need fancy wrappings, except for your skin. These gifts will last, but Paul also says, *Against such things there is no law* (Galatians 5:23). There is no limit. There is no limit to how loving you want to be. There is no limit, so you can be as joyful as you want. There is no law against how much peace you share. There is no limit to how patient and kind and gentle and self-controlled you want to be. So, have fun with it. Be generous.

Give a gift that lasts. Give yourself. Someone needs you.

Unscrambling the Scrambled

During a lunchtime discussion on life, decisions, and consequences, a friend shared an insight he had received from his brother: "You can't unscramble scrambled eggs." We all acknowledged the truthfulness of the statement with nods of affirmation.

Then the comment was made that we spend a lot of time trying to unscramble the scrambled.

Businessmen and businesswomen spend countless dollars and man-hours trying to repair the damage that was done by a careless comment or an oversight in customer service. Apologies can be offered. Promises can be made. But what was done is done. It can't be undone.

Couples say things to one another and then live with the regret of what they said. He apologizes. She accepts, but the words have wounded her heart. She lashes out in anger and immediately realizes that she has hurt him. She tries to take it back, but the damage is done.

Parents do things to their children or for their children and live to wish they could take it back. For the rest of his life he will hear those words ringing in his ears. As long as she lives she will bear the scars of the angry outburst.

The mouths of fools are their undoing, and their lips are a snare to their very lives. – Proverbs 18:7

Church people make decisions then later wish they could undo what has been done. People are hurt. People leave. Souls are damaged. Innocent seekers are confused and discouraged. In retrospect leaders talk in terms of "If we could do that over…", but they can't.

You can't unscramble scrambled eggs.

You were in a hurry and knew you were pushing the speed limit beyond the limits. Just as you thought you better slow down, you top the hill and there the trooper sits with his radar aimed right at you. You see his blue lights. You've been caught. Too late.

When you were a teenager you did things you wish you could forget and wipe from your memory. But you can't. You can't unscramble the mess you have made.

In a careless moment, you gave in to the temptation. You never meant to. But you did. You can't undo what has been done.

You can't unscramble scrambled eggs.

So, what can you do?

I'll let Paul say it: *Not that I have already obtained all this, or have already been made perfect, but I press on to take hold of that for which Christ Jesus took hold of me. Brothers, I do not consider myself yet to have taken hold of it. But one thing I do: Forgetting what is behind and straining toward what is ahead, I press on toward the goal to win the prize for which God has called me heavenward in Christ Jesus.* – Philippians 3:12-14

You can't unscramble scrambled eggs. But you can turn your life over to God and let Him do what only He can do. You can let the eggs stay scrambled and move on. Let Him deal with the scrambled eggs in your life.

Chaos and Peace

Chaos and peace. Evil and good. Tragedy and joy. Disaster and success. Despair and hope. Horror and delight. Sorrow and rejoicing. Ugliness and beauty. Suffering and pleasure. Such is life. At the same time.

Life seems to be falling apart. More demands on your time than you can handle; then more is demanded. When you think there is nothing else that could possibly go wrong, something else goes wrong. Bills are piling up. Tensions are high. At the same time a phone call calms your spirit. A sermon touches your heart. A chapter in the book or an article seems to have been written with you in mind. The Bible passage you have read hundreds of times strangely makes good sense. In the midst of chaos, there is peace.

Life is going great! The family is healthy. Work is good. Your golf game is better than ever. Your boss complimented you on your work. Your child got all A's. Both cars are running well. Your mail includes a rebate you had forgotten about. At the same time, there's an accident. A phone call in the early morning hours. You are dazed. In the midst of peace, there is chaos.

Your ministry is going great. The church is growing. Souls are being saved. Lives are being changed. You know God is doing it, and you are delighted to give Him all the glory. You are just enjoying being along for the ride. At the same time beneath your vision evil is lurking. Waiting for the right time to attack. Temptation is stronger than ever, and you are feeling weaker than ever. Guilt, fear, negativity, anger, and resentment are eating at you. In the midst of goodness, there is evil.

Your ministry is in the pits. Your spiritual life is dry and empty. You are questioning your call. It's been so long since you felt like you were actually helping anyone that you are now considering leaving your post. You are discouraged and frustrated and tired. At the same time an email arrives thanking you for a kindness you showed someone. A phone call from a friend lifts your spirits. At the end of your class one of your students hangs around to say they are getting a lot out of your class and that they appreciate all the time you spend in preparation. In the midst of evil, there is goodness.

This is life. In the midst of the darkest of hours comes a flickering light to remind you to hang on until morning. In the brightest of days there is a shadow that reminds you to be grateful for the brightness of the day. In the midst of unbearable suffering there is a thought of heaven and a day when all suffering ends. In the midst of indescribable joy there is a song that takes you back to sadder days to remind you that there are those around you in great need.

As Jesus prayed in the garden, He battled Satan's evil temptations at the same time. As He visited the home of a friend who had died, He brought hope of the Resurrection. As He moved among the poor, the oppressed, and the blind, He brought riches, freedom, and sight. As He taught his disciples to love, the tempter convinced one to betray Him. As He suffered on the cross, He saved us from our sins. As He died, we gained life. We are alive because He died. We have life "to the full" because He became empty. We die to ourselves so we can live for Him and so that others will follow.

This is life. This is the message of the cross. Perhaps one key to life is to accept this reality, to always be aware of it, and to not get so caught up in one that we forget the other is present.

Are You Listening to Me?

I have recently been involved with our church staff in an administrative project that involved listening to several sales talks. I have had telephone conversations and face-to-face conversations. We have met in my office and on one occasion we traveled to the salesperson for a demonstration. Although we have yet to seal the deal, I have learned a few things that might be helpful for those who are selling products, as well as for those who are interested in sharing your faith.

First, don't assume. I have known for quite some time the dangers of assuming, but the frustrations were brought back to me as I found myself on the other side of the table. The representatives from one company came to my office assuming (apparently) that because we were a church we would want the cheapest equipment and the cheapest deal we could get. Understandably, that is all too typical for churches. Though we are not trying to go for broke, we *are* interested in a quality product. Because of the assumption, we probably will not go with this company.

Sometimes when we talk to people about their relationship with God we assume too much. We may assume that they have a relationship when they do not. We may assume they don't have a relationship when, in fact, they do. We may assume their relationship is at the same spiritual level as ours. It may not be. They may be younger and weaker in their faith. They may be beyond us in our understanding of God. When we assume we run the risk of missing where they are.

Second, explain it to me. One salesperson made a quick visit, dropped off a folder with prices and descriptions of the product, and left. With an enthusiastic handshake and a broad smile, he left saying, "Call me if you have any questions." I did not know enough to know what questions to ask. Needless to say, I did not call.

Sometimes we forget that everyone may not understand our "church" language. I wonder what some people think when they visit our assemblies and hear announcements about "Gospel meetings", "Devos", and sermons on "Propitiation." I suspect they feel much like I did when I traveled to a foreign land and had no idea what was being said and why people were laughing. We sometimes forget that not everyone has been reading the Bible since they could read and taken to church every Sunday and every Wednesday since their parents brought them home from the hospital.

Third, listen to me. Perhaps the most frustrating sales pitch of all was from the two men who asked me what we were interested in, I told them, then they proceeded to suggest a plan that was totally different from what we wanted. I repeated our wishes. They repeated their information. When the bid came, it was more along the lines of what they wanted to sell than what we want to buy.

I fear we do this quite often when we are talking about God, life issues, or getting to know someone. We may ask, "How are you?" But do we listen for a response? Do we really listen for how they are? Or do we assume they are fine or that they are going to give us the same answer we always give: "Fine. And you?"

When I look at how Jesus dealt with people I do not see Him assuming anything. Of course, He could see into a person's heart and knew what they were thinking even clearer than they did. Still He did not assume. I see Him explaining things in such a way than even a child could understand. And I see Him listening to people. He took time to hear their words and to hear their hearts.

We have made a decision on which company and which product. We arrived at the decision for several reasons. The representative did not assume, answered our questions, and listened to our needs. I think the same will happen when we share our relationship with the Lord. Most people do not want us to assume who or where they are in their faith. Most people need some explanation of spiritual matters. Most people want to be listened to.

Let's try it.

A Distracted Mind

In 2001 Russell Crowe starred in the movie *A Beautiful Mind*. The movie tells the story of John Nash, "a math prodigy able to solve problems that baffled the greatest of minds, and how he overcame years of suffering through schizophrenia to win the Nobel Prize" (anonymous). Nash is portrayed as a man tortured by his paranoia and seemingly doomed to self-destruction. The movie was very interesting and won high acclaim, but I have another idea for a movie. My movie is called *The Distracted Mind*.

The Distracted Mind focuses on every day, ordinary, run-of-the-mill Christians who wake up every day with creative intentions to do good deeds, plans to serve mankind, and a commitment to purity and holiness. Unfortunately, the plot takes on a demonic twist as the characters become so distracted that not far into their day they are filled with frustration, discouragement, and feelings of failure and futility.

In one scene, one of the central characters, we will call him Tom, decides his focus for the day will be kindness. He commits to be kind to every person he meets. Before Tom leaves the house, he is faced with issues, people, and circumstances that challenge his commitment to kindness. His wife reminds him that he is taking the children to school (an agreement he had forgotten). She then informs him that she must leave early and therefore he will also need to make their breakfast. In the kitchen scene, Tom almost snaps when he burns the toast and spills the milk, but he reminds himself that his goal for the day is kindness. He maintains his composure through breakfast and during a very rushed drive to school. Unfortunately, a forgotten book bag and an accident two blocks from school are more than he can handle. By the time he reaches his workplace his desire is anything but kindness. His secretary and an early morning sales person soon discover just how far Tom is from any plan to show kindness.

In another scene, Richard is in his office working on an important project. He is preparing to teach a Bible Class. He notices someone walking down the hall and gets up to see who it is. While he is in the hall he notices a bulletin board has been updated so he takes time to read the new items. He hears the sound of someone hammering so he walks further down the hall to check it out. His phone rings so he answers it as he returns to his office. The phone conversation ends so he goes back to his studies at his desk. Just as he opens his Bible to the assigned text his computer signals that a new email has arrived. The rest of his day is pretty much the same.

On the same day, Harry plans an evening with his family. There are no meetings to attend, and he is caught up on his work so that the family can sit down at the table for dinner and conversation and perhaps enjoy a movie together. As he leaves the office he gets a call from his boss asking him to "do him a favor" and he "needs it by 9:00 AM tomorrow." He looks at his watch. Sighs. Calls home to say, "I'll be a little late."

In yet another scene, Mary (Harry's wife) is the victim of the distracted mind. You see Mary is a stay-at-home mom with three small children. Finding time to read, pray, and reflect on God's Word is rare. There have been times when she has almost given up and resolved that, "It's not going to happen." However, one Monday she decides to give it one more try. She gets up early and reads a few verses, but as she begins her prayer her mind wanders. In a few minutes there will be mouths to feed, stories to read, boo-boos to kiss, tears to dry, and bottoms to clean. She takes comfort in the fact that Harry will come home in time to give her a break.

These scenes should be enough to give you the idea that *The Distracted Mind* is a true "reality" show. Though it is doubtful that it will ever make it to the big screen, it certainly makes it into our homes, workplace, and fellowship. To keep our minds fresh and centered on "things above" is a challenge. These New Testament passages may help.

Therefore, I urge you, brothers, in view of God's mercy, to offer your bodies as living sacrifices, holy and pleasing to God — this is your spiritual act of worship. Do not conform any longer to the pattern of this world, but be transformed by the renewing of your mind. Then you will be able to test and approve what God's will is — his good, pleasing and perfect will. – Romans 12:1,2

Your attitude should be the same as that of Christ Jesus, ... – Philippians 2:5

Therefore, holy brothers, who share in the heavenly calling, fix your thoughts on Jesus, the apostle and high priest whom we confess. – Hebrews 3:1

Therefore, since we are surrounded by such a great cloud of witnesses, let us throw off everything that hinders and the sin that so easily entangles, and let us run with perseverance the race marked out for us. Let us fix our eyes on Jesus, the author and perfecter of our faith, who for the joy set before him endured the cross, scorning its shame, and sat down at the right hand of the throne of God. Consider him who endured such opposition from sinful men, so that you will not grow weary and lose heart. – Hebrews 12:1-3

Having a mind that is centered on spiritual things and free of distractions may seem to be an impossible dream. It can happen. You can do it. It is not easy and takes training, but it's not impossible. The Enemy does not want it to happen, but it can happen. Ask for God's guidance, allow His Spirit to work in you, and renew your mind. In the midst of the stresses of your busy days, in the middle of a crisis, and as you deal with the unending demands of your day, you can find peace and enjoy an "undistracted mind."

May God bless you and center your thoughts on Him.

A Blank Page

I turn on my computer. Open my word processing application. Open my file for last week's article. Change the date and number and delete the title. What's left? A blank page. Sometimes the words come easy. Sometimes it is a struggle. Every time it begins with a blank page.

Every article begins as a blank page. Usually there is a thought in my head that has not yet made it to the page. Gradually the words flow from the idea in my head to the keys on my keyboard and eventually to the page on my screen. It begins as a blank page.

Every sermon begins as a blank page. The text is determined. The passage is read and digested. Eventually a few thoughts are transferred from the margin of my Bible, my PDA, or my journal onto the page which I will use when I deliver my sermon. It begins as a blank page.

Every day begins as a blank page. The night is over, and the alarm sounds. My eyes open. My head clears, and I begin to focus on what lies ahead. A meeting. A class. An appointment. A visit. Phone calls to make. Some are pleasant; some are not so pleasant. By the time my feet are on the floor my schedule for the day is set. It begins as a blank page.

Every phone call begins as a blank page. The telephone rings. I check the caller ID. I flip the phone open. The conversation begins with the usual pleasantries, and the conversation progresses then ends with the usual pleasantries. It begins as a blank page.

Every email begins as a blank page. I pull up my email program. Read my unread mail. Click on the "New" button. Select the addressee. Type my message. It begins as a blank page.

Every job begins as a blank page. The application is completed. The initial interview is scheduled and completed. The job is offered and accepted. The alarm blares early in the morning. The first day begins. It begins as a blank page.

Every relationship begins as a blank page. The couple makes eye contact. They have a brief conversation. He makes a phone call. They make a date. They make another date. They make another date. The relationship grows and matures. It begins as a blank page.

Every life begins as a blank page. We grow and develop. We learn and mature. We listen and talk. We work, and we play. We get hurt, and we heal. We sin and repent. We give and receive. We cry, and we laugh. It begins as a blank page.

Because of this decision we don't evaluate people by what they have or how they look. We looked at the Messiah that way once and got it all wrong, as you know. We certainly don't look at him that way anymore. Now we look inside, and what we see is that anyone united with the Messiah gets a fresh start, is created new. The old life is gone; a new life burgeons! Look at it! – 2 Corinthians 5:16-17 (*The Message*)

We begin as a blank page. We can write whatever we choose on our blank page. When our page gets full or stained or cluttered or damaged, because of God's grace we can begin again as a blank page.

Maybe It's Time to Live

Maybe it's time we started to live the life God created us to live. We've pretended long enough. We've talked about it long enough. We've talked *around* it long enough. Maybe it's time we stopped doing so much talking and started living the life.

But you are a chosen people, a royal priesthood, a holy nation, and a people belonging to God, that you may declare the praises of him who called you out of darkness into his wonderful light. Once you were not a people, but now you are the people of God; once you had not received mercy, but now you have received mercy.

Dear friends, I urge you, as aliens and strangers in the world, to abstain from sinful desires, which war against your soul. Live such good lives among the pagans that, though they accuse you of doing wrong, they may see your good deeds and glorify God on the day he visits us. – 1 Peter 2:9-12

Maybe it's time we did as Peter suggests and live like we are a chosen people, live like we are part of the royal priesthood, live like we are a holy nation, and live like we belong to the Lord. Maybe it's time we began living like we were called out of the darkness and into the light. Maybe it's time we began living like we are a people of God. Maybe it's time we began living like we have received mercy.

Maybe it's time we accepted the fact that we are aliens and strangers in the world and started abstaining from sinful desires. Maybe it's time we started living such good lives that though someone may accuse us of doing wrong, they can only see our good deeds and end up glorifying God.

Maybe it's time we started letting our light shine before men so that they can see our good deeds and glorify God.

Maybe it's time we began living like the salt of the earth. Maybe it's time we became the light of the world.

Maybe it's time we started taking care of the widows and orphans.

Maybe it's time we began to love the Lord our God with all our heart, our soul, our mind, and our strength. Maybe it's time we began to love our neighbor as ourselves.

Maybe it's time we began to be known by our love for one another.

We have talked enough. We have waited long enough. We have gathered and shared enough information. Maybe it's time we began to live the life.

Trusting His Timing

One of the features of my new mobile phone is a clock that allows you to see the time in multiple time zones, set an alarm, use a stopwatch, and time an event. When I take a walk I usually set the timer for about fifteen minutes short of the length of time I want to walk so that I can decide the route for the last part of the walk. For instance, if I plan to walk for an hour I will set it for 45 minutes. Invariably, I will check the timer a number of times before the alarm sounds.

Is this thing working? Did it sound and I did not hear it?

Has there has been a malfunction?

Thus far, the alarm has never failed to work. I have never walked an extra hour by accident. The device has never failed to perform as it is designed to do. Yet, there is a feeling of distrust in the clock.

The same thing happens as I walk through life trying to live on God's time-table.

I have read the instructions from His word about trusting God. I am listening to Him, praying for His will to be done. I believe that He is working even though I cannot see it. I know that He is in charge. I know that nothing will happen that escapes His view. I know that He cares for me. I know that He has always and will always deal with me according to His justice and goodness. However, there are still times when I have difficulty trusting His timing.

I have discovered three realities about trusting His timing.

First, trusting His timing is sometimes hard. There are times when I eagerly lay my cares down, but then I decide not to wait for God to work and pick them back up again. There are other times when my concerns must be ripped from my hands. My doubts and fears take over: What if He does not listen? What if He hears the wrong thing? What if He chooses to act in a way that I do not like? Or worse, what if He chooses not to act at all? I have swallowed hard when He responded with "No," and I have laid awake at night wrestling with His answers that appear to be "Not now."

Second, trusting His timing is sometimes easy. There are times when waiting for God to work His plan is easy. Laying my concerns at the feet of the Lord and leaving them there comes naturally. I have experienced answered prayer soon after making the request. I receive his "Yes" with joy and gratitude. I receive His "No" with patience and trust.

Third, whether easy or difficult I have learned over my life and from His word that the Father's timing is *always* right.

Solomon said it this way: *He [God] has made everything beautiful in its time. He has also set eternity in the hearts of men; yet they cannot fathom what God has done from beginning to end.* – Ecclesiastes 3:11

You may be in a waiting time. Waiting for the answer. Waiting for direction. Waiting for peace. Waiting for hope. Waiting for healing. Waiting for victory. Doubt and uncertainty may have set in. You may be left with questions and fears.

Whatever you are waiting for, trust His timing – it is always right.

He has made everything beautiful in its time.

Then I Understood

The first part of Psalm 73 contains the writer's thoughts that reveal his station in life and the condition of his heart. First, he says, *my feet had almost slipped; I had nearly lost my foothold. For I envied the arrogant when I saw the prosperity of the wicked* (v. 2-3). Then he lists many of the things about the arrogant. They have *no struggles, healthy and strong, free from common burdens and human ills...always carefree, they increase in wealth* (v. 4-5).

He goes on to admit that as he focused on those people and their way of life he began to think about what a wasted life he had lived. *Surely in vain have I kept my heart pure; in vain have I washed my hands in innocence* (v. 13). The more he thought about it, the more oppressive it became. *When I tried to understand all this, it was oppressive to me* (v. 16).

How often do our minds drift into the realm of the lifestyles of the rich and famous? How often do we allow envy to obscure our vision and blind us to the reality of what is genuinely good, truly wholesome, and spiritually healthy? We wish, we fantasize, and we waste our lives longing for what we do not have and what we do not need. Something significant usually has to occur to reshape our mental processes and help us regain a healthy perspective on life.

The psalmist describes what did it for him, *till I entered the sanctuary of God; then I understood their final destiny. Surely you place them on slippery ground; you cast them down to ruin. How suddenly are they destroyed, completely swept away by terrors! As a dream when one awakes, so when you arise, O Lord, you will despise them as fantasies. When my heart was grieved and my spirit embittered, I was senseless and ignorant; I was a brute beast before you* (v. 17-22). (This may be the first Biblical mention of the infamous "slippery slope." Notice that this reference is something totally different from how this reference is usually used.)

As he began to de-clutter his mind his vision also improved: *Yet I am always with you; you hold me by my right hand. You guide me with your counsel, and afterward you will take me into glory. Whom have I in heaven but you? And earth has nothing I desire besides you. My flesh and my heart may fail, but God is the strength of my heart and my portion forever. Those who are far from you will perish; you destroy all who are unfaithful to you. But as for me, it is good to be near God. I have made the Sovereign Lord my refuge; I will tell of all your deeds* (v. 23-28).

Being in the presence of God changes things. Here's how *The Message* says it, *Till I entered the sanctuary of God; Then I understood their final destiny. Then I saw the whole picture:...*

The *Amplified Bible* says, *then I understood [for I considered] their end.*

The *Contemporary English Version* says, *Then I went to your temple, and there I understood what will happen to my enemies.*

When we are in the presence of God we see things differently. When we are in the presence of God we understand things. When we are in the presence of God we see the whole picture.

If you are feeling that life is passing you by, go to the sanctuary of God. If you find yourself envious of the "in" crowd, go to the sanctuary of God. If you wish you were in their shoes more often than you are glad you are in yours, spend some time with God and allow being in His presence to help you gain a better perspective on who He is, who you are, and how He cares for you. Spend time in the presence of God, then you'll understand.

Just a Taste

The weather forecast was for snow. Children snuggled under the covers and eventually drifted off to sleep to dream of building snowmen, making snow angels, and no school the next day. Parents were tuned in to the list of closed schools running constantly at the bottom of the screen and frequently peeked out the window to see if anything was falling. Daylight revealed only a dusting. There was just enough to give a taste of a real snow.

While having lunch with a group of friends I was offered just a taste of Key Lime Pie. The taste made me want more. I ordered my own slice.

When I pop a bag of popcorn my wife usually says, "I'll have just a taste." Someone else might take a taste and pop another bag of popcorn. (SIDE NOTE: The late Smookie Norvell, one of the cats we had years ago, would not settle for just a taste. He always wanted a good serving of popcorn.)

Dad placed his daughter in the swing made just for her. He pushed her and she giggled in utter delight. She wanted more. "Don't stop, Daddy!"

It had been a wonderful weekend in a luxurious hotel. The time passed so quickly as we took advantage of all the amenities, made the most of every moment, and enjoyed every conversation. Checkout time came much too soon. We wanted it to last longer.

The whole family had gathered for the holiday celebration. There was an abundance of food, the chatter was pleasant, and the love was overflowing. Someone said, "I wish we could have more times like this."

The group from church had traveled several miles to attend the weekend conference. Everyone came in need of spiritual refreshment. All left satisfied. The worship was spirited and God-focused. The speakers were encouraging and convicting. The fellowship of believers was heart-warming. As we gathered for the last time before departing someone said, "Surely this is just a taste of what Heaven will be!"

Just a taste.

Sometimes it is a song. Sometimes it is an aroma. Sometimes it is a word or a phrase. That's all it takes to send us across the miles and through the years to a time that was or to a time that we hope someday will be. All it takes is a taste and we're back home, in a foreign land, on the beach, standing on the top of a mountain, or in the company of the one we love.

For three years, the followers of Jesus watched, listened, and learned from the Master. At times, they were confused and left to wonder what was ahead for them as He spoke of the coming Kingdom. As He prepared to leave them He made them a promise:

Believe me when I say that I am in the Father and the Father is in me; or at least believe on the evidence of the works themselves. Very truly I tell you, whoever believes in me will do the works I have been doing, and they will do even greater things than these, because I am going to the Father. And I will do whatever you ask in my name, so that the Father may be glorified in the Son. – John 14:11-13

After all they had seen as one of Jesus' disciples - the miraculous healings, the dead who were given life, the teaching, the compassion, the courage - He tells them, "You are going to do those things and even greater things. What you have seen and experienced is just a taste of what you will see and do."

Paul made a similar statement to the Ephesian church:

Now to Him who is able to do exceedingly abundantly above all that we ask or think, according to the power that works in us, to Him be glory in the church by Christ Jesus to all generations, forever and ever. Amen. – Ephesians 3:20-21

In this life we are given just a taste of what will be one day. Our best days in this life are only a glimpse of what it will be when we are in the presence of the almighty God. When we experience something is this life that we think must be like heaven, it's only a taste of what is to come.

(Thirty-five years ago this evening my wife and I stood before a gathering of our friends and family committing our lives to one another for as long as we should live. On that evening we both thought, "This is the best day of our lives." Looking back on those thirty-five years we now realize that was just a taste of what was to come. Thank you, Kim, for thirty-five years. What we have experienced during the last thirty-five years and what we are experiencing now is just a taste of what we will one day experience when we cross the threshold into glory. Happy Anniversary!)

One Thing I Know

In the ninth chapter, John tells the story of the man blind from birth as Jesus gives him his sight. The man invokes considerable conversation concerning the reason for his blindness, then the reason for his newfound ability to see. It is clear from the text that Jesus' purpose for the miracle was to demonstrate His power as the Son of God, as well as to make it possible for God the Father to become more visible.

As the story unfolds the man is brought before the leaders of religion for questioning. They question his integrity: "Were you really blind?" They question his parent's integrity: "Was your son really born blind?" They question him about Jesus: "Surely he is a sinner. Don't you agree?"

He replied, "Whether he is a sinner or not, I don't know. One thing I do know. I was blind but now I see!" – John 9:25

The man's response is refreshingly simple. "All I know for sure is that I was blind and now I can see."

He's not concerned about the details of how it happened. He's not concerned about the motives of the one who healed him. He's not really concerned about what these keepers of the law think about it. His concern is that he was blind and now he can see.

We can learn much from this man. It is not necessary to have all the answers to be a powerful influence. Our message of faith does not have to be complicated or outrageous. Our testimony does not have to be overly dramatic or littered with scandal. Our story simply needs to be honest, from the heart, and centered around God.

I was blind, but now I can see.

I was sick, but now I am well.

I was rejected, but now I am loved.

I was empty, but now I am full.

I was dirty, but now I am clean.

I was weary, but now I am refreshed.

I was crippled, but now I can walk.

I was dead, but now I am alive.

My family was falling apart; now we are one.

Our church was breaking apart; now we are united.

Our marriage was about to end; now we are in love again.

God has given each of us a story of being healed, a story of faith, a story of hope, a story of salvation, a story of reconciliation and restoration, or a story that reveals God's mighty power and faithfulness.

I was lost, but now I'm found.

Don't worry about explaining it all, trying to use descriptive words, or whether or not people believe what you say. Just tell your story of what God has done or is doing in your life. Just tell what you have seen and what you have heard. Just tell what you know.

Tell the one thing that you know is true.

Missing the Meal

I have never been one for missing meals, especially family meals. If the family is together, I like to be there. On this day, however, due to a recent surgery I am missing a meal (actually several meals). The meal I am missing today is not one of my favorite recipes or impressive culinary creations. The meal I am missing today is the meal that takes place when the family of God gathers around the table to remember what the Lord has done for us.

"For I tell you I will not drink again from the fruit of the vine until the kingdom of God comes."

And he took bread, gave thanks and broke it, and gave it to them, saying, "This is my body given for you; do this in remembrance of me."

In the same way, after the supper he took the cup, saying, "This cup is the new covenant in my blood, which is poured out for you." – Luke 22:18-20

The significance of the meal extends beyond the small piece of bread or the tiny cup of grape juice that I take from a shiny silver tray every Sunday morning during the communion service. It is more than the breaking and the sipping and the songs. The meaning of the meal goes deep into the heart of what it means to be a family and what it means to be connected. Surely that is what Jesus had in mind when He initiated the meal.

He never meant for it to become routine or ordinary or boring. He meant for it to be a reminder for us that we are not alone, that we will never be alone, and that He will be with us always. He meant for us to remember that the body that assembles on these ordinary Sunday mornings has the potential to change the ordinary day into something extraordinary.

When we gather for the meal we have the opportunity to see our brothers and sisters in the shadow of the cross and realize that we have come together as forgiven sons and daughters of the King of Kings. When we share the meal, we have the opportunity to remember the suffering that Jesus experienced so that we can be forgiven sons and daughters. We have the opportunity to say "Thank You" to the One who died for us. We have the opportunity to rejoice with one another, to share our hearts with one another, and to experience genuine communion – real oneness.

Because of the frequency of the event and the distractions of life, I have not always experienced the presence of the Lord in dynamic and real ways. There are times when travel or illness has prevented being physically present at the meal. But the meal is always significant. The conversation before and after the meal is significant. The fellowship of believers that accompanies the meal is significant. The expressions of love for the Lord and devotion to one another are significant. The meal and all that goes with it are significant because of the One who issued the invitation for us to gather with Him for the meal. I cannot fathom receiving an invitation to the meal from the Lord of Lords and ignoring it or turning it down. I do not like to think about the family gathering for a meal and me not being included. Jesus couldn't imagine that either.

If all goes well next week I will again gather with my brothers and sisters – those that assemble locally and those scattered around the world – for the meal of remembrance and hope.

Today I am missing the meal. I've missed it before. Chances are I will miss it again. But today I miss it and that is significant.

Starting to Quit

I recently read an article by Scott Couchenour titled *Be A Quitter – 25 Ways*. The article reminded me of these words of Jesus, *"Therefore do not worry about tomorrow, for tomorrow will worry about itself. Each day has enough trouble of its own."* – Matthew 6:34 And *"To those who use well what they are given, even more will be given, and they will have an abundance."* – Matthew 25:29 (*New Living Translation*)

The article reminded me of Paul's words in Philippians, and in particular this passage: *I'm not saying that I have this all together, that I have it made. But I am well on my way, reaching out for Christ, who has so wondrously reached out for me. Friends, don't get me wrong: By no means do I count myself an expert in all of this, but I've got my eye on the goal, where God is beckoning us onward—to Jesus. I'm off and running, and I'm not turning back.* – Philippians 3:12-14 (*The Message*)

The article reminded me of some things I need to quit doing, so, I am adding a few things to Couchenour's list.

I am starting to quit wishing my life away. All the "What if..." and "If only..." and "I wish..." thoughts must go. Actually, it is more than just the thoughts, it is when thoughts become journeys into fantasyland that waste time and energy. Today is all that I have. Not yesterday. Not tomorrow. I am living today.

I am starting to quit allowing what other people do, say, or think or what they do not do, say, or think dictate what I do, say, or think. My words need to be God's words. *Do not let any unwholesome talk come out of your mouths, but only what is helpful for building others up according to their needs, that it may benefit those who listen.* – Ephesians 4:29

My attitude needs to be that of Christ. *Your attitude should be the same as that of Christ Jesus.* – Philippians 2:5

My actions need to be God's actions: *Who, being in very nature God, did not consider equality with God something to be grasped, but made himself nothing, taking the very nature of a servant, being made in human likeness. And being found in appearance as a man, he humbled himself and became obedient to death—even death on a cross!* – Philippians 2:6-8

I am starting to quit waiting on forgiveness. I know God forgives me. I know that once I ask another person to forgive me and have done what I can to reconcile, I have done all I can do. When someone does me wrong, if I do not forgive and forgive quickly I only do more harm to myself, and harboring a grudge may create an opening for the Enemy to enter my heart. *Give us today our daily bread. Forgive us our debts, as we also have forgiven our debtors. And lead us not into temptation, but deliver us from the evil one.* – Matthew 6:11-13

I am starting to quit moving in such a hurry. When I move too quickly I miss things, I miss people, and I forget what is important. When I slow down I can see God more clearly, I can love God more dearly, and I can follow God more nearly (Go ahead and sing if you want). *Be still, and know that I am God.* – Psalm 46:10

I am starting to quit believing that I am stronger than I really am. I am weak. He is strong:

Three times I pleaded with the Lord to take it away from me. But he said to me, "My grace is sufficient for you, for my power is made perfect in weakness." Therefore I will boast all the more gladly about my weaknesses, so that Christ's power may rest on me. That is why, for Christ's sake, I delight in weaknesses, in insults, in hardships, in persecutions, in difficulties. For when I am weak, then I am strong. – 2 Corinthians 12:8-10

What needs to go on your "Starting to Quit" list? It is probably either time to quit, about time to quit, or well past time for quitting.

Why wait?

Tis the Season for Gentleness

Like it or not, ready or not, the holiday season is upon us. Thanksgiving, Christmas, and New Year's Day are no doubt the big three holidays of our culture. From mid-October until we pass into a new year, we are thrust into holidays that emphasize gratitude, the birth of Jesus, and starting over. Not a bad combination of spiritual themes. If we allow ourselves, these days can provide opportunities for us to share our faith, express our hope, and offer valuable instruction on living the life of a follower of Jesus. Or we can moan and groan, whimper and whine, and waste the blessings and miss the open doors.

This passage, Philippians 4:5, offers wise counsel for handling the stresses and strains of the season: *Let your gentleness be evident to all. The Lord is near.*

These two short sentences seem to fit: gentleness and God's presence. His nearness reminds us of the gentleness with which He deals with us. His gentleness reminds us that He is near. When we focus on gentleness, we display His nearness to others. When others experience our gentleness, they may be reminded of His presence. As we live with the knowledge of His nearness – that He could come soon – being gentle seems a natural byproduct. *Let your gentleness be evident to all. The Lord is near.*

With a gentle awareness of the Lord's presence, I offer these suggestions that may bring more joy to the world and more peace on the earth.

When you are standing in a long line at the check-out stand in the department store, running late, and in a hurry, remember to "Let your gentleness be evident to all. The Lord is near."

When you are in a line of traffic that is not moving at all, and the guy in the sporty little car zooms past you on the shoulder and then turns on his blinker hoping you will let him in, remember to "Let your gentleness be evident to all. The Lord is near."

When your children ask for the thirteenth time in the last hour, "How many more days until Christmas?" remember to "Let your gentleness be evident to all. The Lord is near."

When your husband calls to say he is working overtime...again...to make a little extra money for Christmas, remember to "Let your gentleness be evident to all. The Lord is near."

When your in-laws call to tell you they have decided to come to your house for the entire week between Christmas and New Year's Day, remember to "Let your gentleness be evident to all. The Lord is near."

When you are stressed out because the item that is going to make the difference in this being an okay Christmas and a great Christmas is completely sold out, remember to "Let your gentleness be evident to all. The Lord is near."

When you have shopped, faced the crowds, and fought traffic only to walk in the door and your husband says, "Honey, what's for dinner?" remember to "Let your gentleness be evident to all. The Lord is near."

When the older man in line in front of you decides to use the self-check-out for the first time ever, remember to "Let your gentleness be evident to all. The Lord is near."

When people are rude, unkind, inconsiderate, irritating, annoying, disrespectful, obnoxious, and downright mean, remember to "Let your gentleness be evident to all. The Lord is near."

When you have messed up and disappointed yourself by losing your patience and losing your cool, remember to "Let your gentleness be evident to all. The Lord is near."

When you are tired of shopping, tired of wrapping presents, tired of fixing meals, tired of relatives, and really tired of people in general, remember to, "Let your gentleness be evident to all. The Lord is near."

Let your gentleness be evident to all. The Lord is near.

As One Who Serves

Jesus said to them, "The kings of the Gentiles lord it over them; and those who exercise authority over them call themselves Benefactors. But you are not to be like that. Instead, the greatest among you should be like the youngest, and the one who rules like the one who serves. For who is greater, the one who is at the table or the one who serves? Is it not the one who is at the table? But I am among you as one who serves." – Luke 22:25-27

We are a privileged people. As you read these words you must know that you are among the most privileged people on the earth. You can read. If you read these words with the assistance of some form of reading aid (glasses, contacts, optical surgery), you are among the most privileged people. You have some form of good medical care. If you read these words on a computer, iPad, or Smartphone, you are among the most privileged people. You are part of a very small percentage of the world's population.

We are a privileged people. If you have electricity in your home, you are among privileged people. If you have running water in your home – hot and cold, sanitary and fresh – you are among privileged people. If you have a refrigerator in your home, if you have access to a washing machine, or if you own or have access to an automobile, you are among privileged people.

We are a privileged people. If you have had more than one meal to eat in the last twenty-four hours, you are among the privileged people of the earth. If you have a television in your home, you are among the most privileged people. If you have relatively easy access to a well-stocked grocery store, you are among the privileged people of the earth.

We are a privileged people. If you have the freedom to go to work, earn a living, and feed your family, you are one of the privileged people. If you enjoy the freedom of attaining an education you are among the most privileged people on the earth. If you have never been restricted in how you worship, where you worship, and who you worship, you are among the privileged people.

We are a privileged people. What will we do with our privileged status? We can demand our rights. We can boast of our privileges. We can hoard our privileges. Or we can refuse to demand our rights. We can acknowledge that everything we have is a gift from God. We can share what we have been given.

We are among privileged people, but our Lord tells us that we are not to act like privileged people. We are to use our privileged status to be the servants. The most privileged of all came to earth and surrendered His privileged nature to live as one who serves.

We are privileged people. May we follow the example of our Lord and live as one who serves.

Take Nothing

When Jesus had called the Twelve together, he gave them power and authority to drive out all demons and to cure diseases, and he sent them out to preach the kingdom of God and to heal the sick. He told them: "Take nothing for the journey—no staff, no bag, no bread, no money, no extra tunic. Whatever house you enter, stay there until you leave that town. If people do not welcome you, shake the dust off your feet when you leave their town, as a testimony against them." So they set out and went from village to village, preaching the gospel and healing people everywhere. – Luke 9:1-6

Go back and read the first part of what Jesus told the Twelve when He sent them out to preach the Kingdom and heal the sick: "Take nothing for the journey—"

When I read those words, I thought: "I am sure glad that Jesus does not call us to do that today." Or does He? I began looking for the passage that assures me that He indeed does not call us to that kind of life. Where is that passage? Maybe it was in *The Message*:

He said, "Don't load yourselves up with equipment. Keep it simple; you are the equipment. And no luxury inns—get a modest place and be content there until you leave. If you're not welcomed, leave town. Don't make a scene. Shrug your shoulders and move on."

Nope. Not there.

Thinking we can surely reach a compromise, I have a conversation with the Lord.

Me: "Can You tell me again what all we will need when we go out to talk to people about You?"

The Lord: "Take nothing for the journey."

Me: "Excuse me. Nothing?"

The Lord: "Take nothing for the journey—no staff, no bag, no bread, no money, no extra tunic."

Me: "Nothing?"

The Lord: "Nothing. Take nothing for the journey—no car, no suitcase, no snacks, no extra clothes, no extra pair of comfortable shoes, no money, no credit cards, no iPhone, no iPad, no MacBook Pro. No extra pens. No books to read. Nothing to write on. Nothing."

Me: "You can't be serious. Do you realize how much stuff I carry with me everywhere I go?"

The Lord: "I do realize it. Take nothing."

Me: "Really? Nothing?"

The Lord: "Really. Nothing. Nothing. Take nothing for the journey—no car, no suitcase, no snacks, no extra clothes, no extra pair of comfortable shoes, no money, no credit cards, no iPhone, no iPad, no MacBook Pro. No extra pens. No books to read. Nothing to write on. Nothing."

Me: "Whoa! Nothing? Not even my favorite coffee mug?"

The Lord: "They probably have nice coffee mugs where you are going. If not, you will be okay."

Me: "Hmmm. Can I think about it? This is hard!"

The Lord: "You can think about it if you want, but my instructions are not going to change."

Me: "Lord, what if I take…"

The Lord: "Tom, you have all you need. I am with you. I am all you need. It is time to go. Go."

As I ponder His words, I pray:

"Father, help me hear Your call, and Your promise. Help me to trust You. Help me to believe that I have what I need. Help me stop questioning, help me stop looking for excuses, and help me stop looking for a way to compromise. Father, help me to put all my efforts and all my resources and all my energy and all my abilities and all my ideas and all of my words in Your hands and know that You are all I need. Father, help me take nothing but You and go do what You have empowered me to do."

Swing Your Swing

The week leading up to and including my sixtieth birthday was filled with sharing memories, eating my favorite foods, receiving cards, gifts, and messages from friends and family, and some times of deep reflection on where I have been and where I am going. The time has been well spent and the good wishes have been appreciated. (By the way, it was March 1 for those who need to know and forgot to send a gift. It is not too late. I am still accepting.)

One question that has been asked numerous times is: "Well, how does it feel to be sixty?" My typical answer has been: "A lot like fifty-nine." Physically, mentally, emotionally, and spiritually in reality it is no different. And yet it is. Six decades. Sounds like a long time, seems like a long time, yet it also seems very brief. As one Facebook friend stated, "It seems like I just wished you a happy birthday."

Part of the reason this birthday seems different is that in my mind sixty years implies some level of wisdom. From my perspective, I have always looked at men and women who were sixty and above with at least some degree of respect. My reasoning being if they have lived this long they surely have learned something, so I can learn something from them. Obviously, that is not always true. Some appear to have lived their sixty-plus years and managed to bypass the accumulation of wisdom.

So, as the day approached and passed I continued to look for that wisdom that I could pass along to those coming behind me (and maybe even some of those who are ahead of me), that would make their journey easier and more enjoyable.

The insight came during a commercial break of a recorded program about the one called the greatest golfer of all time, and is narrated by another of golf's greatest.

Swing your swing. That is it. Arnold Palmer and Dick's Sporting Goods said it well.

Swing your swing. Live your life. Live the life you have been given.

Not the life you wish you had. Or the life you think you should live. Live the life you have been given. Use your talents. Do what you were created to do.

Long before the commercial, the company, the game of golf, and any of the great golfers, God used his servant Paul to live the message of being who you were created to be, then offered these instructions on how to function well within the body:

But in fact, God has placed the parts in the body, every one of them, just as he wanted them to be. – 1 Corinthians 12:18

Now you are the body of Christ, and each one of you is a part of it. – 1 Corinthians 12:27

So, my bit of wisdom to you is this: Swing your swing. Be you. God created you to be you. Learn from other people. Glean from the experience and wisdom of those who have gone before you. But be you.

If you are a teacher, teach the way you teach. If you are a singer, sing with your voice and your music. If you are an athlete, play your game your way. If you are a preacher, preach the message God is giving you and share the message the way God has equipped you to share it.

Although God has placed and will place very gifted and talented people in your life and along your path, do not try to be them. Some of those you respected may even try to push you into their mold or shape you into someone they admire and respect. Resist the pressure. Swing your swing. Play your way. Live your life. Use your talents. Develop your gifts. Follow God your way. Swing your swing.

Torn Between the Two

Have you ever been at a crossroads in life where your choices were all good? If you go down one road, you are confident that good things are going to happen. If you go down the other road, you are equally confident that good, perhaps better, things will happen. You want this, and you want that.

Your trust in God is strong. He has always been faithful to His people, He has never left you alone, and He has proven over and over that He is worthy of your trust. There is no doubt that regardless of your decision, He will walk with you, He will carry you if necessary, and He will deliver you in His way and on His timetable. You know it.

That is Paul's conflict as he writes to his beloved friends in Philippi.

Yes, and I will continue to rejoice, for I know that through your prayers and God's provision of the Spirit of Jesus Christ what has happened to me will turn out for my deliverance. I eagerly expect and hope that I will in no way be ashamed, but will have sufficient courage so that now as always Christ will be exalted in my body, whether by life or by death. For to me, to live is Christ and to die is gain. If I am to go on living in the body, this will mean fruitful labor for me. Yet what shall I choose? I do not know! I am torn between the two: I desire to depart and be with Christ, which is better by far; but it is more necessary for you that I remain in the body. Convinced of this, I know that I will remain, and I will continue with all of you for your progress and joy in the faith, so that through my being with you again your boasting in Christ Jesus will abound on account of me. – Philippians 1:18-26*

Paul says, "For to me, to live is Christ and to die is gain."

I am torn between the two. I want, I prefer, to leave this body and dwell with God. But it seems that being here with and for you is best. I am torn between the two. "For to me, to live is Christ and to die is gain."

I am torn between the two. On those days when decisions are difficult, questions outweigh answers, and rest seems beyond reach, I want to leave this earth. On those same days, I am reminded of relationships, old and new, where God has allowed and continues to allow me to have significant influence, and I want to stay here a little longer.

I am torn between the two. There are situations that require so much of me that I want to escape, run away, find a hole and crawl in it. In the same instant, I can see that these circumstances provide a challenge, a promise of growth, and the opportunity to develop my faith.

When it comes time to leave my children and granddaughters and return home, no matter how long the visit, I am torn between the two. I love my family. I feel extremely blessed for any amount of time I get to spend with them. I love our conversations. I love the openness and honesty we have developed. I love watching our granddaughters as they develop new skills, expand their horizons, and make new discoveries. I also love the ministry God has blessed me with. I love the people with whom I share this ministry. I love seeing God open doors of opportunity to share His message of love and forgiveness. When it comes time to leave and go home, I am torn between the two. I want to stay, and I want to go. I want to go, but I also want to stay.

Like Paul I desire one thing, but it is necessary that I hear God's voice and follow His leading so that those God has placed in my path may be blessed and encouraged, and so that I may receive blessings and encouragement from them.

As we are in this world and endeavoring to be followers of Jesus we will be torn between the two (or more) options, situations, and opportunities that God places before us. It is where we are. It is who we are. I suppose as we come to the end of our time in this world we will be torn between staying here with loved ones and going home to be with the Father.

Like the Apostle, "For to us, to live is Christ and to die is gain." May we walk in His Spirit and live courageously, boldly, and joyfully all the days of our lives!

The Attitude

Relationships! Whew! To say relationships are difficult to cultivate and maintain is a major understatement.

A significant portion of our lives is consumed with trying to create, understand, and improve our relationships. We read books. We attend lectures and seminars. We ask friends for advice. We seek the wisdom of those more experienced. We lose sleep over relationships. We stress over relationships. We cry over broken relationships, and we shed tears of joy when relationships mature and last for years.

Marriage relationships are difficult. Parent and child relationships stretch us to our limits. Friendships keep us perplexed. Spiritual relationships can be extremely disappointing due to our expectations that come from the fact that we are dealing with people of like faith and similar thinking.

Relationship gurus offer a variety of suggestions for improving our relationships. Better communication. Spend more time together. Spend better time together. For men: Talk more. For women: Talk less. For both: Listen more and better. For parents: Ask the right questions, ask questions in the right way, watch your tone when asking questions, and don't ask too many questions.

In writing to a group of Christians who were dealing with some critical relationship matters that were threatening the spiritual harmony of the community, Paul offered simple but profound advice: *Think of yourselves the way Christ Jesus thought of himself.* – Philippians 2:5 (*The Message*)

That's easy, isn't it? Just think about yourself the way Christ thought about himself. No problem.

Another version called it an attitude: *Have this attitude in yourselves which was also in Christ Jesus.* – Philippians 2:5 (*NASB*)

Another calls it a mindset: *In your relationships with one another, have the same mindset as Christ Jesus.* – Philippians 2:5 (*NIV*)

The mindset, the attitude of thinking like Christ involves becoming a servant. The original language indicates it is the lowliest of the servants. To live like Jesus, to treat others like Jesus treated people, requires us to empty ourselves of our natural tendencies and replace them with the tendencies of God.

To be like Jesus we must replace our arrogance with humility. To be like Jesus we must practice a level of obedience and submission beyond anything that would come to us naturally. It requires an obedience that would enable us to give our very life should it come to that.

Here is how Paul described it:

Who, being in very nature God, did not consider equality with God something to be used to his own advantage; rather, he made himself nothing by taking the very nature of a servant, being made in human likeness. And being found in appearance as a man, he humbled himself by becoming obedient to death — even death on a cross! Therefore, God exalted him to the highest place and gave him the name that is above every name, that at the name of Jesus every knee should bow, in heaven and on earth and under the earth, and every tongue acknowledge that Jesus Christ is Lord, to the glory of God the Father. – Philippians 2:6-11

Relationships! Whew! What do you do? Start here: Have the attitude of Jesus.

No More Second Guessing

Do everything readily and cheerfully — no bickering, no second-guessing allowed! Go out into the world uncorrupted, a breath of fresh air in this squalid and polluted society. Provide people with a glimpse of good living and of the living God. Carry the light-giving Message into the night so I'll have good cause to be proud of you on the day that Christ returns. You'll be living proof that I didn't go to all this work for nothing.
– Philippians 2:14-16 *(The Message)*

What would it be like to live in a world, in a church, in a workplace, or in a home where no second-guessing is allowed?

You would never remind everyone who will halfway listen that if you were the President of the United States you would never make the decision he made.

When teachers make an assignment, there would be no chorus of "Are you serious?" coming from the class.

When a referee makes a call, no coach would yell from the bench, no player would stomp down the court, and no fan would scream at the top of his lungs, "Are you crazy? That is a horrible call!"

When the boss makes an assignment, employees would simply smile and get busy completing the task.

When a parent asks a child to get busy cleaning his or her room, without comment the room would get cleaned.

When a lifelong friend informs you that she is leaving her job for mission work in a poverty-stricken country on the other side of the world, the only response you would give is that of encouragement and complete support.

When your daughter says she is in love and wants to get married, the only thing you would say is that you love her and cannot wait for the wedding.

When the elders make a difficult but prayer-soaked decision, there would be no threats of leaving or resistance to their authority.

When a husband tells his wife he cannot continue to work under the stressful conditions of his job and needs to make a change, she would hug him and says she is supportive.

Those might be some of the things we would experience if we were to live in a world, in a church, in a workplace, or in a home where no second-guessing is allowed.

Am I dreaming? Is this foolish thinking? Am I naive? Are you second-guessing me?

Apparently, the Lord felt it is not an impossibility since He guided Paul to write those words. It does not matter what kind of Bible you read from, the message is the same:

Do everything without grumbling or arguing – Philippians 2:14 (*NIV*)

Do all things without grumbling or disputing (*NASB* and *ESV*)

Do all things without murmurings and disputings (*KJV*)

Can you imagine such a world? Can you imagine being a person that never second-guesses, or grumbles, or complains, or argues? This text is not written only to that annoying person who always second-guesses you; it is also written to you. Do not second-guess that. It is true. It is also written to me.

What would it be like to live like that? You would *Go out into the world uncorrupted, a breath of fresh air in this squalid and polluted society. Provide people with a glimpse of good living and of the living God. Carry the light-giving Message into the night. (The Message) Then you will shine among them like stars in the sky. (NIV)*

I think it is possible. I think it is worth trying. I think a world like that would be absolutely wonderful. Even if you think differently please do not second-guess me.

The Mature View

In Philippians 3 Paul is describing his past, present and future life. He has already expressed how he has let go of his past life, the good and the bad, because he has found something far more valuable — Jesus. He continues to share his station in life in the next section by admitting that this process of letting go of the garbage is an ongoing task. *Not that I have already obtained all this...* (v. 12)

The fact that he is not there does not discourage him. (Of course, neither does being in prison or being away from the people he loves.) He keeps trying. He is honest with us when he says, "I'm not there yet. But I keep trying." It is a constant battle to forget, leave behind, and press on toward the goal.

Remember the goal is Jesus. He keeps reaching for Jesus. He keeps stretching forward toward Jesus. He keeps moving toward Jesus. He keeps longing to be more like Jesus. Not there yet; but still moving. He is not going to stop until he reaches the goal.

Then Paul makes an interesting statement: *All of us, then, who are mature should take such a view of things.* (Philippians 3:15) I presume the "view" refers to his not having yet arrived.

Apparently, Paul was often confronted with, bothered by, and criticized by groups who claimed to be mature. Their proof of maturity came from their achievements in keeping the law. So, he is taking a jab at them here by saying somewhat sarcastically that if they were really mature they would know this and would have this view. "Of course, anyone who is really mature would already know this."

Do not allow his jab at the opposition distract you from his point. The mature view: I'm not there yet, but still moving forward.

I think Paul is teaching us that part of being mature is knowing we are not as mature as we think we are...even when we are mature.

He goes as far to say, "Follow my example" and follow those who live like I do. There are those who would lead you off in another direction; do not follow them. We have a higher calling. We have a greater goal than following the rules. We have a more important role to play in the world than being right.

Keep your eye on the goal. Keep reaching. Do not allow these other folks to discourage you.

He would say the same thing to you. Especially if you have someone, some "mature" person telling you how you are supposed to live. Especially if that life involves getting it all right all the time. Especially if you are trying that life and finding that you are unable. You keep messing up. You keep coming up short. You want to quit.

Please don't quit. Please keep your eye on the goal — Jesus. Read Hebrews 12. Read the Sermon on the Mount (Matthew 5, 6, and 7). Read Philippians again.

You can do it. You can keep trying. You can keep pressing on toward the goal. You can. You can. You can. I believe in you. Paul believes in you. More importantly God believes in you and has sent the Holy Spirit to dwell with you and in you. It is the mature view.

You've got this!

It is Time for a Little Gentleness

Let your gentleness be evident to all. The Lord is near. – Philippians 4:5

As I write these words we are consumed with the holidays and all that goes with it. Children are barely able to contain their excitement. Parents are scrambling to make sure the right presents are purchased, wrapped, and carefully placed under the tree for Christmas morning. Merchants are working overtime to makes sure shelves are stocked and employees are taking good care of the sometimes-desperate customers.

At the same time stress levels rise as couples wonder how they are going pay their medical bills. Department store clerks do their best to satisfy the overstressed and demanding customers impatiently waiting their turn in the never-ending lines at the cash registers. Production team supervisors demand more from their team members than they can possibly accomplish.

At the same time protests continue throughout the country illustrating the racial tension that still exists. Political leaders argue over the best plan to keep the government in operation for another year. Each party will boast of their cooperative spirit and how much quicker an agreement could have been reached had it not been for selfishness of the other party. Threats of foreign terrorist attacks, tortured and murdered prisoners, as well as reports of our own government using unsanctioned methods to receive secret information.

It is time for gentleness to be evident. Remember the Lord is near. Remember this season is about the Lord coming to earth to be near to us. It is time for a little gentleness.

I am not suggesting a sentimental gentleness that simply smiles to avoid a confrontation. I am not suggesting a gentleness that covers a broken heart with a sugary sweet insincere greeting.

The gentleness I am suggesting flows from a heart that has been transformed by the presence of God. The gentleness I am suggesting comes as a result of being touched by the compassion of Jesus. The gentleness I am suggesting is not manufactured to make a good showing but is a natural by-product of being filled with the Spirit of God. The gentleness I am suggesting is possible when one has been comforted by the gentleness of a spirit-filled loved one.

It is time to let gentleness be evident among Christians when we disagree with other Christians on matters of minor importance, and on matters of major importance. It is time to let gentleness be evident between members of the same church when things do not turn out the way we had hoped they would. It is time to let gentleness be evident when we hear something that surprises and disappoints us about another follower of Jesus — gentleness, not assumptions or accusations.

When rebellion is evident, it is time to let gentleness be equally evident. When disappointment is evident, it is time to let gentleness be equally evident. When complete failure has occurred, been discovered and confessed, it is time to let gentleness be abundantly evident. When people are demanding, rude, disrespectful, selfish, and generally unkind, it is time to let gentleness be miraculously evident.

The Lord is near. It is time to let gentleness be evident to all.

Think on These Things

Would you like to end your year on a high note? Here is a simple and easy suggestion. It is not original with me. The Holy Spirit put the words in Paul's mind, Paul put them to paper, and I share them from my computer.

Finally, brothers and sisters, whatever is true, whatever is noble, whatever is right, whatever is pure, whatever is lovely, whatever is admirable — if anything is excellent or praiseworthy — think about such things. Whatever you have learned or received or heard from me, or seen in me — put it into practice. And the God of peace will be with you. – Philippians 4:8-9

Sometime over the next few days consider trying this.

Think. Take some time, fifteen minutes, thirty minutes, an hour or two and think. Think about the last twelve months. Think about how God has blessed you, surprised you, amazed you, challenged you, corrected you, or changed you. Think. Stop and be quiet and think.

Think specifically about these things.

As you reflect, think about the things you have learned, observed, or experienced that are true. The Bible. The love of a spouse, a parent, a friend, and God's love.

As you reflect think about noble things. Things that are of great value and of high character. Think about what is dignified. Think about what is awe-inspiring. Think about things that are above and beyond your imagination.

Think about things that are right. Think about what is right about your family. Think about what is right about the world. Think about what is right about your church. Think about what is right and avoid focusing on what is wrong. Think about what has been right about your year.

Think about what is pure. There is so much impurity in the world. Focus on things as they are supposed to be, not tarnished or watered down. Think about the purity of a newborn baby. Think about the pure love of a newly married couple. Think about the purity of a clear mountain morning. Think about the purity of a singer's voice when she hits the notes perfectly.

And do not ignore the lovely. Think about lovely things. Think about that lady in your church when you were young — always dressed in the most appropriate fashion, her personality and spirit matching her wardrobe. Think about that tree down the street that had the perfect shape, filled with the brilliant orange leaves.

When I hear the word admirable I see faces. I see the faces of men and women who have inspired me by their words, their actions, their encouragement, their ethics, and their spirituality. Think about those people this week. If possible, contact them and tell them you are thinking about them and admire them.

Because you can see mediocrity running rampant, why not choose to think about things that are excellent. Think about an event you attended this year and came away thinking and commenting, "That was excellent!" Maybe it was a concert. Perhaps it was a sporting event. It could have been service at a favorite restaurant.

As you bring your reflection time to an end, think about things that deserve your praise. Think about your co-worker who did a great job on a difficult project, then tell them. Think about the performance of the young lady during her recital, then praise her. Think about the view of the ocean waves, then thank the Creator of the land and the sea. Think about that sunset that took your breath, then thank the One who made the sun, the moon, the stars, the sky, and your eyes to see them, then praise Him. Think about the One who created everything you see, hear, feel, taste, smell, experience, in the past, in the present, and in the future, then lift holy hands to praise the Lord God Almighty.

I hope you will spend some time this week thinking on these things, and I hope you welcome the new year with renewed faith, restored hope, and refreshed spiritual passion.

The Shadows We Cast

Maybe it was because it was a beautiful and cool fall, early-winter afternoon. Maybe it because it was Friday afternoon. Maybe it was because the sun was going down and casting long shadows from the evergreens, the oaks, and the maples. Maybe it was the music I was listening to. Maybe it was just a fluke. Maybe it was my age and where I am in life. Whatever the reason, this afternoon walk was a time of reflection on the week that was ending, the people I had interacted with, the sermon I was formulating for Sunday, and the next article I would write.

The combination of the angle of the setting sun and the shadows being cast by the trees across the hills, the open fields, the ponds, and the path where I was walking was too much for this amateur photographer to resist, so I snapped a few quick shots from my phone. The old club house, pro shop, tennis court, and pool house are gone. The difference in the landscape is amazing. The leaves that two weeks ago were spectacular in color have mostly turned brown and blown away, leaving the trees embarrassingly bare. From the shadows in the distance down the hill a deer stood motionless to make sure I did not move in her direction.

Having reached the end of my outward walk I was on the way back when I stopped to get this one shot across the water with the sun to my back. Focused on the pond and the hillside in the distance I did not notice that the snapshot included my shadow, long and stretched thin in the foreground of the picture. It captured the afternoon perfectly. "What a long shadow I am casting this afternoon!" I thought.

As Jesus walked the earth, His shadow, His presence, brought good news to the poor, freedom to the imprisoned, restored sight to the blind, and release for the oppressed. He brought life to lifeless, hope to the hopeless, and joy to the joyless. His shadow, His presence, fell upon the angry, the hurting, the lonely, the sinful, the broken, and the forgotten. His shadow, His presence, is significant and makes a difference in the life of all who will allow it.

That image, coupled with those thoughts, nudged my pondering from an image of a shadow on the ground to the shadow of my life. What kind of shadow have I cast with the life I have lived? What kind of shadow do I cast with the life I am living now? As the light of the Son shines over me, does my shadow impact another life for the better? Is the life I am living providing a moment of beauty, a moment of peace, a moment of encouragement, a moment of joy for those whose lives I am touching? Or it is just a shadow?

I wondered about my shadow, my presence. What impact is my shadow, my presence, having on those around me? Do those upon whom my shadow falls sense a peace in me that passes understanding? Do those upon whom my shadow falls feel a presence that will bring refreshment to their souls? Are those upon whom my shadow falls aware of the presence of God?

Today my shadow will be cast across more lives than I can fathom. Yours will, too. May the shadow we cast bring good news to the poor, freedom to the imprisoned, restored sight to the blind, and release for the oppressed. May the shadow we cast this week offer life to the lifeless, hope to the hopeless, and joy to the joyless. May the shadow we cast, may our presence, fall upon the angry, the hurting, the lonely, the sinful, the broken, and the forgotten in a way that is significant, that makes a difference in their lives.

Your Last Words

Within a few days we will say farewell and goodbye to another year. As we end a year and welcome a new one, many will spend at least some time developing plans and making resolutions for the coming year. There will be news stories about the first baby born in the hospitals. There will likely be stories about the first couples to be married. And sadly, some news programs will report the first death of the new year. Over the next week we will be experiencing and talking about all kinds of firsts that occur as the first days of the new year pass.

Instead of focusing on the *first* things, I would like to spend the space of this message thinking about the *last* thing. What is the last thing you will talk about this year? It is a fairly common tendency among families and friends to share some of the most important and meaningful information during the last few minutes of our time together. We may chit chat throughout the visit. We may spend much of our time on trivialities until we are ready to walk out the door.

Parents will often end their visit with their children with words like, "Be careful." "Call us when you get home." "Do you have enough cash?" In our family we have always tried to say, "I love you" before we leave, even if it is for a trip to the grocery store.

So, these are the words I want to leave you with as the year comes to an end.

Now this is eternal life: that they know you, the only true God, and Jesus Christ, whom you have sent. – John 17:3

This is my desire for you. That you know the only true God and Jesus Christ. My goal for *Until Hope Returns* is to help you know Jesus. It is not my desire to tell you about heaven or how wonderful it will be. It is not my desire to tell you about how important it is for you go to and be involved in a church or spiritual community. It is not my goal to help you get it right with how you worship. It is my desire to help you know Jesus.

I know of no more important questions that I can ask you than these:

Do you know Jesus? Do you understand that Jesus came to earth, lived on earth, died, and rose again so that you could be forgiven of all your sins? Do you know that if you know Jesus, you have eternal life, because He is eternal life?

The year's end is near. Do you know Jesus? What are your last words?

When?

On Sunday morning I preached from the judgement scene passage in Matthew 25:31-46. I admitted that every time I dwell for very long on this passage I become angry, sad, disappointed, and discouraged because we so often fall short of ministering to the least of these as the sheep are rewarded for doing.

During my sermon I included this piece of writing that I have periodically read and shared in various settings for forty years.

<u>You Seem So Holy</u>

I was hungry, and you formed a humanities group to discuss my hunger.

I was imprisoned, and you crept off to your chapel and prayed for my release.

I was naked, and in your mind you debate the morality of my appearance.

I was sick, and you knelt and thanked God for your health.

I was homeless, and you preached to me of the spiritual shelter of the love of God.

I was lonely, and you left me alone to pray for me.

You seem so holy, so close to God

But I am still very hungry — and lonely — and cold.

- Author Unknown

My challenge to the assembly and my challenge to this electronic congregation is when?

When will we — God's people — realize and take care of the least of these – the hungry, the lonely, the helpless, and those in bondage?

When will we — God's people — realize that our work is not about bigger buildings, deeper pockets, more elaborate programming, or larger numbers in our assemblies?

When will we — God's people — realize that our mission field is lost people, not people of faith who are attached to a community of faith that goes by a name different than ours?

When will we — God's people — acknowledge that we tend to be easily distracted from our purpose by trying to do too much, build a reputation, or gain political influence?

When will we — God's people — understand that turning on our lights, providing comfortable seating, and setting out coffee and donuts is not all there is to ministering to the least of these?

When will we — God's people — realize that demanding that the Ten Commandments be posted in public places, complaining about prayer being unlawful in public schools, protesting outside abortion clinics is not the same as feeding the hungry, housing the homeless, and spending time with a lonely person?

When will we — God's people — realize that ministering to the least of these means that it doesn't matter how they are dressed, how they smell, the kind of language they may use, or the amount of ink on their body?

When will we — God's people — understand that ministering to the least of these is not limited exclusively to ministers, priests, clergy, elders, deacons, and credentialed professionals?

When will we — God's people — realize that ministering to the least of these may require us to interact with people of another color, another culture, or another political party?

When will we — God's people — realize that ministering to the least of these may involve sacrifice, inconvenience, and unpleasantness, not merely writing a check or dropping some cash in a basket?

When will we — God's people — realize that ministering to the least of these is not our legal obligation that insures our ticket into heaven, but the natural response to being counted as one of God's children?

When will we — God's people — realize that ministering to the least of these is the same as ministering to Jesus and is the same thing that Jesus did and would do if He were here today?

When?

Soon I hope.

When I Am Weak

Complete this sentence: When I am weak…

When I am weak I feel like a failure.

When I am weak I want to quit.

When I am weak I want to give up.

When I am weak I want to cry.

When I am weak I want to run away.

When I am weak I feel lost.

When I am weak I think my life is a waste.

Paul said, *When I am weak, then I am strong.* (2 Corinthians 12:10)

It is rare for us to hear anyone admit a weakness in our day, much less take pride in our weakness like Paul does. You almost never hear an athlete admit a weakness. When a celebrity admits a weakness, it is usually only after a scandal has been uncovered. Certainly, not in our current political conversation will you hear any of the contenders admit a weakness.

Paul had reached a level of spiritual maturity where he not only admits his weaknesses, but takes pride in them (2 Corinthians 12:8-10). A man, who most readers and believers of Scripture consider a spiritual giant, takes pride in being a failure.

What is the message? What are we to learn from Paul's example?

Simply and profoundly this: God is our strength.

When you feel that you are weak that is when God will fill you with His strength.

When you have failed, God will give you victory.

When you want to quit, God will help you go on.

When you are crying, God will renew your Spirit.

When you feel lost, God will be your home.

When you think your life is a waste, God will show you your value.

When you are weak, God's grace will be sufficient.

If this week is anything like last week, or the week before, or the week before that, there will be something that happens this week that makes you realize that you cannot handle everything by yourself. It could be a family disturbance. It could be an upset customer. It could be a disgruntled employee. It could be a bad report from the doctor.

Whatever it happens to be, you may find yourself feeling weak, helpless, and powerless. When that happens listen closely and carefully, and you will hear God saying, "My grace is sufficient for you." Trust that. Lean into that. Know that is true.

Thank Him, and when you are sharing your story include this statement: "When I am weak, then I am strong."

A Quiet Life

Make it your ambition to lead a quiet life: You should mind your own business and work with your hands, just as we told you, so that your daily life may win the respect of outsiders and so that you will not be dependent on anybody. — 1 Thessalonians 4:11-12

"A quiet life?" Some of you read that phrase and thought, "Dream on, Dude! Ain't happening! You can talk about living a quiet life all you want, but you don't know the world I live in. There is nothing quiet about it!"

Unfortunately, I hear statements like that too often. Unfortunately, I also find myself thinking along those same lines and using similar language.

There are two words in the sentence that appear to be contradictory: "ambition" and "quiet life." We rarely put those two words together.

When we think of ambition we think of climbing the corporate ladder, getting to the top before anyone else, winning at all cost, being the very best, being a high achiever, and accumulating the most. Ambition is often spelled B-U-S-Y. Ambition speaks of hustle and hurry.

When we think of a quiet life we hear Jesus say, "*Come to me and I will give you rest.*" (Matthew 11:28) We hear the psalmist say: "*Be still and know that I am God.*" (Psalm 46:10) The quiet life reminds us of peaceful waters, green pasture, and a restored soul.

When we think of ambition we are reminded of the disciples arguing over, "Who is the greatest?" When we think of the quiet life we are reminded of Jesus going off by Himself to a quiet place.

When we think of ambition we have visions of the President. When we think of the quiet life we see images of a father fishing with his son on the bank of a pond.

When we think of ambition we see the corner office with a spectacular view of the city. When we think of the quiet life we see Granddaddy sitting in his rocker on the front porch.

When we think ambition we often think hard-working and successful. When we think of the quiet life we often think laziness and failure.

Is the quiet life feasible in our day? It must be, and Paul provides three simple guidelines for living the quiet life.

Plan for it. The quiet life will not just happen. It must be your ambition. It must be your goal. You must plan for it. You will not wake up one morning and suddenly your world has become quiet. You will need to work at living a quiet life. There will be things you must stop if you are going to live a quiet life. You will need to shut down and shut out some of the noise in your life, get rid of some of the clutter in your life, and focus on what really matters. To have a quiet life you must desire a quiet life.

Mind your own business. Wow! What a difference that will make! Do not read that statement like siblings would say it to each other: "Mind your own business!" Read like a loving spiritual parent would say it to their spiritual son or daughter who is trying to be the person God wants them to be: "Just mind your own business. It's not your responsibility to straighten out the rest of the world. You have plenty to do taking care of your own business. Don't borrow frustration from someone else. Just mind your own business." Social media would certainly change if we started minding our own business. Conversations between friends would sound different. That does not mean you ignore the needs of other people. Paul has covered that in other places. As a general rule, mind your own business.

Do your own job. Work with your hands. What have you been trained to do? Do that. What are you most passionate about? Do that. Do it well. Work hard at what you are gifted to do. You cannot do someone else's job and still do yours well. If you are teacher, then be a teacher. If you are a preacher, then be a preacher. If you are an artist, be an artist. If you are a police officer, be a police officer. If you serve coffee, then serve coffee.

The quiet life often escapes us not because it is unachievable, but because we make excuses, because we enjoy being (or appearing) over-worked and over-committed, and because we simply refuse to make it our ambition. It is your choice. Is it important? Is it possible? God thought it was important enough to include in His Book. Maybe this week you will experience the quiet life.

The Complaining Stops Here

The *Jesus Calling* entry for October 9 hit me right between the eyes. I told the Lord that in my own prayer journal entry. The reason it hit so hard is that it was not only the words from Sarah Young, or the words she included in her writing from the Lord, but these have been my words.

I have spoken them. I have taught them. I have preached them. I have counseled with them. I have written about them. As I read them again in this setting and in the context of my circumstances, the power of the words penetrated in my heart like never before.

What are the words? They are found in Philippians 2:14-15, *Do everything without complaining or arguing, so that you may become blameless and pure, children of God without fault in a crooked and depraved generation, in which you shine like stars in the universe.*

Earlier in the day's thoughts Young had written: "You have been on a long, uphill journey, and your energy is almost spent." And I said, "Yes, I have, and my energy is almost spent."

Then I read further, "Though you have faltered at times, you have not let go of My hand. I am pleased with your desire to stay close to Me." And I said, "Yes! Thank You, Lord, for noticing."

Then I read further: "There is one thing, however, that displeases Me: your tendency to complain." And I said nothing. I could not believe what I was reading. I was stunned. I was frozen in the silence of the morning and by the convicting nature of these words. Eventually I said, "You are right, Lord." (Excerpt From: Young, Sarah. *Jesus Calling.* Thomas Nelson, 2004.)

I finished the reading and at the bottom of the page were the words, *Do everything without complaining or arguing, so that you may become blameless and pure, children of God without fault in a crooked and depraved generation, in which you shine like stars in the universe.*

The words of God have spoken and I have heard them, so today the complaining stops. At least that is my goal...again.

As I have "been on a long, uphill journey", and as I have spent so much of my energy, I have enjoyed a season of complaint. It has felt good. I have felt justified. Those who have listened have affirmed my justification and kindly listened to my complaints. It stops today.

How can I complain about anything when others have lost everything due to the storm that has been slowly crawling up the East Coast?

How can I complain about anything when I have enough food in our refrigerator and pantry to feed us for days?

How can I complain when I can sit in a comfortable chair where I have access to more excellent reading material and information than I can possibly ever consume?

How can I complain when I live in a beautiful part of the world in a beautiful time of the year and where I am reminded multiple times every day that I am loved by people and by the Lord Almighty?

As I understand the passage I cannot "shine like a star in the universe" unless the complaining stops. The Word of God speaks. The power of the Word has penetrated my heart. The complaining needs to stop. It might as well stop with me. You can join me if you like. If you choose not to do so, I'll try not to complain.

P.S. I do reserve the right to sometimes make sarcastic comments about sportscasters and news reporters.

No Bullying

In the introduction section to Peter's letters, *The Message* says this about Peter:

"In the early church, his influence was enormous and acknowledged by all. By virtue of his position, he was easily the most powerful figure in the Christian community. And his energetic preaching, ardent prayer, bold healing and wise direction confirmed the trust placed in him.

"The way Peter handled himself in that position of power is even more impressive than the power itself. He stayed out of the center, didn't "wield" power, maintained a scrupulous subordination to Jesus. Given his charismatic personality and well-deserved position at the head, he could easily have taken over, using the prominence of his association with Jesus to promote himself. That he didn't do it, given the frequency with which spiritual leaders do exactly that, is impressive. Peter is a breath of fresh air.

"The two letters Peter wrote exhibit the qualities of Jesus that the Holy Spirit shaped in him: a readiness to embrace suffering rather than prestige, a wisdom developed from experience and not imposed from a book, a humility that lacked nothing in vigor or imagination. From what we know of the early stories of Peter, he had in him all the makings of a bully. That he didn't become a bully (and religious bullies are the worst kind) but rather the boldly confident and humbly self-effacing servant of Jesus Christ that we discern in these letters, is a compelling witness to what he himself describes as 'a brand-new life, with everything to live for.'"

One line that stands out in this description is: "From what we know of the early stories of Peter, he had in him all the makings of a bully."

We hear about and are appalled by bully stories. We cringe at stories of the damage done by bullies. We are horrified when we hear a story about a teenager who attempts to take her life as a result of being bullied at school and in social media. We are heartbroken by stories when the attempt is successful.

One would think that a spiritual community would be a safe place where bullying would not be a problem, but too often that is not the case. How sad it is to hear about church leaders who abuse their power and influence by bullying those under their care. Spiritual bullying may result in the loss of faith, a separation from their church, or walking away from a relationship with God all together.

If you have ever dealt with a religious bully, you will agree with Peterson's comment that "religious bullies are the worst kind."

In the early part of chapter 5 Peter demonstrates his understanding of the better way by offering wise counsel to those who serve as spiritual leaders:

I have a special concern for you church leaders. I know what it's like to be a leader, in on Christ's sufferings as well as the coming glory. Here's my concern: that you care for God's flock with all the diligence of a shepherd. Not because you have to, but because you want to please God. Not calculating what you can get out of it, but acting spontaneously. Not bossily telling others what to do, but tenderly showing them the way.
– 1 Peter 5:1-3 (*The Message*)

You see more proof of Peter's understanding of the Jesus style as he explains how to avoid being a spiritual bully:

And you who are younger must follow your leaders. But all of you, leaders and followers alike, are to be down to earth with each other, for—

God has had it with the proud,

But takes delight in just plain people.

So be content with who you are, and don't put on airs. God's strong hand is on you; he'll promote you at the right time. Live carefree before God; he is most careful with you. – 1 Peter 5:5-7 (*The Message*)

Peter suggest two attitudes.

First, *Be down to earth with each other.* Why? Because *God has had it with the proud, but takes delight in just plain people.*

Second, *Be content with who you are, and don't put on airs.* Why? Because

God's strong hand is on you; He'll promote you at the right time.

This is not easy. Most of us have a desire for people to think like we think. Those of us who are considered spiritual leaders may have to really fight those same tendencies. We may, at times, try to persuade our friends, co-workers, and those under our care to adhere to our way of thinking and our style of living. If our way is not accepted, we may resort to intimidation or forced conformity.

Peter says...Jesus says...Just be you. Let others be who they are. Live your life. Be a guide to others who look to you as an example. Encourage them. Teach them the Jesus life. Love them as they grow and just be plain people. Don't be a bully! Because God knows how to deal with bullies.

You Were Born To Be You

Who am I? What was I created to be and to do? Why am I here? Do I have a purpose? Does God have a plan for my life? These are questions some of us struggle with from time to time. Some of us struggle with them all the time.

How about you? Ever wonder why you were placed on this earth? Does another year passing make you sad because it means you still do not know why you were born?

Maybe Romans 12 will offer some help.

For by the grace given me I say to every one of you: Do not think of yourself more highly than you ought, but rather think of yourself with sober judgment, in accordance with the faith God has distributed to each of you. For just as each of us has one body with many members, and these members do not all have the same function, so in Christ we, though many, form one body, and each member belongs to all the others. We have different gifts, according to the grace given to each of us. If your gift is prophesying, then prophesy in accordance with your faith; if it is serving, then serve; if it is teaching, then teach; if it is to encourage, then give encouragement; if it is giving, then give generously; if it is to lead, do it diligently; if it is to show mercy, do it cheerfully. (v.3-8)

Insight Number One: Maybe we think too much about ourselves. In verse 3 Paul instructs us *Do not think more highly than you ought…* Maybe one way to read that would be, "Don't spend so much time thinking about yourself." Use sober or clear-headed judgment about yourself. Maybe we spend too much time trying to figure ourselves out when we should spend more time focusing on God and what He is doing, and how we can fit into His plan

Insight Number Two: God's plan for us is not necessarily a puzzle to be solved. It is mysterious. But the puzzle has been solved. *I have become its servant by the commission God gave me to present to you the word of God in its fullness—the mystery that has been kept hidden for ages and generations, but is now disclosed to the Lord's people. To them God has chosen to make known among the Gentiles the glorious riches of this mystery, which is Christ in you, the hope of glory. —*

Colossians 1:25-27

Christ in you, the hope of glory. That is a major part of the reason you are here, to allow Christ to be revealed in you. That happens when you have surrendered to Him. That happens when you have made your life a living sacrifice.

Insight Number Three: You were born to be you. God makes it clear that we are all different but we are all joined to be one. We all have different things to give but we make up the one body. We cannot be someone else. We do not have their gift. Although we may have similar qualities as our parents, our siblings, or our closest friends, we are not them. We were not created to be them, or like them. We were formed in our mother's womb to be us. We are to be part of the Body of Christ as designed by God and as He designed us.

You were born to be you. That is where you will be your best. That is where you will flourish. So, be who you were born to be – you.

A Lesson from Larry the Bug Guy

We have had a problem with ants. They keep coming back. When the pest control service people came for the regularly scheduled application we mentioned that we had seen several ants around our kitchen sink and on the cabinets in that area. They sprayed and said, "Call us if you see any more ants."

We saw more ants. We called. They suggested, "Try vinegar and water, and if you still see ants, call us." We tried vinegar and water. We continued to see ants.

We called. The technician returned and used a different chemical. "That should take care of them, but if you see any more call us."

We continued to see more, and more, and more. We called again. A new "Bug Man" came armed to wage war against the ants. When he walked in the door he exuded confidence and seemed excited about the battle. He began by catching one ant, smashing it between his thumb and forefinger and sniffing it to determine "the type of ant we are dealing with." With great enthusiasm, he explained that each ant gives off a special scent. Although he told me, I do not remember the type "we are dealing with." He then proceeded to explain his technique for killing the ants, the chemical he was using, and how it worked. He shared that the ants hunt for food, then communicate with one another once they've discovered some.

After applying the new dose, he began to watch and share how they "are taking the bait" and insisted that I come see a particular group that had swarmed and congregated just above the dishwasher. I'm pretty sure he let out a "Yessir!" at this point.

I thanked him for his determination and knowledge. He thanked me for our business, once again explained the nature of the ant, explained what he had done and how it works, and assured me that "This should take care of the problem."

As he walked to his truck I was reminded of a lesson, not a new lesson,

150

but an old and familiar lesson: We have all been created by God and none of us are exactly the same.

The first verse of the Bible that introduces the creation story in Genesis 1:1 says, *In the beginning God created the heavens and the earth.* As the story unfolds we see the detail and the uniqueness of every creature that God created. He created us all, and He created us all exactly like He wanted us to be. Ants, humans, dogs, and beautiful trees covered in the brilliant colors of autumn.

Thank you, Larry, the Bug Man, for letting me watch you and listen to you and once again be reminded of what a good thing it is that God created us all to be different. No wonder when God finished His creation He said, "This is good."

Let's Just Be the Church

This is my plea: Let's just be the church.

You may begin reading and think, "Man, this guy is angry!" I am not (and if you say that again I may unfriend you on Facebook). That was a joke. I am not angry. I am not bitter. I am not one of those "against everything" people. The goal of my preaching, teaching, writing, and counseling is to help people know Jesus and follow His teachings. If you do not believe that look at my Twitter profile (@TomNorvell). That means it has to be true, right? I am for doing everything within our power and using everything available to us to help people know Jesus and follow his teaching.

I am not angry, but I am tired. I am tired of our pretending to be the church but not living like we are the church. I am tired of our playing silly and ridiculous games that make people think we are the church but failing to follow through with the loving message of God.

At times it appears that we are more committed to trying what is trending to get people into our buildings than we are to being what we need to be when we interact with people. We sometimes seem more concerned about convincing people that we are right, they are wrong, and they better join our team, than we are of loving them like they are and where they are. Sometimes it appears that we have forgotten who we are.

We are not...

A civic club.

A social club.

A country club.

A coffee shop.

A fast food restaurant.

A resort.

A discount department store.

An entertainment center.

A complaint department.

A recreational facility.

A political party.

A judicial system.

There is nothing wrong with any of those businesses and organizations. They all serve a good purpose in our communities. I am not against any of them. I am not suggesting that we are better than any of those businesses or organizations, nor am I ignoring the fact that we can learn much about connecting with people from these businesses and organizations. But they are not the church. We are. We should not expect them to be what God has called us to be.

Let's just be the church!

Let's just be what Jesus told us we are.

Jesus said, "*You are the salt of the earth. But if the salt loses its saltiness, how can it be made salty again? It is no longer good for anything, except to be thrown out and trampled underfoot. You are the light of the world. A town built on a hill cannot be hidden. Neither do people light a lamp and put it under a bowl. Instead they put it on its stand, and it gives light to everyone in the house. In the same way, let your light shine before others, that they may see your good deeds and glorify your Father in heaven.*" (Matthew 5:13-16)

Living as light and salt is different.

Living as light and salt is bringing good things to people. The good news. Good attitudes. We are good neighbors. We are good hosts and hostesses. We are good people. We make life better for people around us.

Living as light and salt is surprising people by loving them, being patient with them, and going the second and third mile with them.

Living as light and salt is not giving up on people even when they fail again and again and again.

Living as light and salt is forgiving them even when they don't ask for it or deserve it.

Living as light and salt is using language that encourages, lifts up, and refreshes people around you.

Living as light and salt is being generous with people who do not expect you to be generous with them, and more generous than you are normally.

Living as light and salt is listening when you prefer to talk and sometimes talking when you would prefer to remain silent.

Living as light and salt is protecting the weak, helping those who are helpless, and defending the defenseless.

Living as light and salt is walking with and in the Spirit, dumping the garbage in our lives, and leaving it behind.

Living as light and salt is refusing to play foolish and stupid religious games and instead getting serious about imitating God.

Living as light and salt is loving God and His people.

This is my plea: Let's just be the church.

The Fifth Last Time

I mowed the lawn at the house we recently moved from for the fifth last time. We listed our house last fall and were confident it would sell. So, as winter approached I mowed the lawn with confidence that it would be the last time. It was not.

Spring came; the grass grew; the house had not sold; I started mowing. I mowed through the spring, then through the summer, and then early fall arrived, and I was still mowing. We signed the papers on the sale and were expected to close within two weeks, so I mowed thinking that would be the last time. The closing was delayed, so I mowed again for the third last time, then again, and finally last week I mowed for the fifth last time. I am optimistic (again) that this last time was the last time. We'll see.

As I finished up and swept off the driveway, I thought of other things that are done multiple last times.

There was the time in college when we thought, "This is the last of these lectures I will ever have to sit through." A low grade (a really low grade) gave us the opportunity to repeat the class (American Literature for me) the next semester.

There is that habit of eating too much, or eating those late-night snacks, or eating whether you are hungry or not. "I will never eat that much food again." "I am not going to eat that late in the day ever again." It worked...until the next time...and then the next.

There are those sins you have asked forgiveness for over and over again. "That's the last time I will click that site." "That's the last time I will talk like that." "I am going to learn to control my temper." It worked. Until the next time.

In sports we make similar promises. "I'll never hit a shot like that again." "I'll never swing at a pitch that far outside again." "I'll never let that guy drive around me toward the basket again." Then you did it again. Then you did it again and again...then you did it again.

Then there are all those times when we said we were going to change

155

our conversation. "I am not going to gossip ever again." "I am going to stop being so negative and cynical and criticize so much." "That is the last time I am going to get caught up in 'the sky is falling and the whole world is going to the dogs' conversation." Then there's the next last time, and the next, and still another last time.

Our friend, Peter, had some trouble with this. He told Jesus he would go with Him wherever He wanted him to. Jesus cautioned him on making such a bold claim, then told him he would deny Him three times before the morning. I suspect when he denied Jesus the first time he promised he would never do it again. He did it again. And he did it the third time. (Mark 14:27-72)

The exceptionally good news is that after those three denials, Jesus offered him a completely restored relationship. (John 21:15-19) He did that because God is a God of second chances, third chances, fourth chances, and as many as it takes. He does not give up on us.

So, if you find that you are on your first or second or third or fourth last time of doing something, or not doing something, keep trying. Maybe, just maybe, the next time will really be the last.

It Does Not Seem Like a Big Deal

It did not seem like a big deal. We were invited to an event, so we went. We enjoyed the gathering and were well received. The people who invited us could not stop thanking us. As we left the event, they thanked us. Later that night we received a text thanking us again. The next morning we received another text thanking us again. It did not seem like a big deal, but to these people it was a really big deal.

It is what I do. I am a counselor. I listen to people; I try to show compassion and offer godly wisdom when possible. It does not seem like a big deal. To a person who is hurting it apparently is a big deal. I have received letters, notes, emails, texts, phone calls, handshakes, hugs, and face to face conversations thanking me for doing what I do.

He probably has no idea what an impact he had on me. He was a basketball coach; I was a very average junior high kid who wanted to play. I later came to know him better as a godly man with a family, successful in his business, and active in the community and his church. His example has stayed with me all these years. He probably has no idea what a big deal it was for him to be kind and encourage that average junior high kid.

He probably did not think it was a big deal. He was my seventh-grade math teacher. That was the year my mother died. I was having a difficult time. He knew it. He showed a sad, scared, and confused seventh grader considerable kindness and grace as he helped me finish the school year with decent grades. I still remember it fifty-one years later. To him it probably did not seem like a big deal.

They may have never realized what a big deal it was for them to be so kind to me. I was just the high school boy dating their daughter. They showed that high school boy an incredible amount of graciousness by feeding me more times than I could recall, taking me to places I would have never gone, introducing me to pizza, and being there when I had questions about faith and church and life. They were just being who they were – wonderful Christian people. Little did they know that the high school boy who was dating their daughter was watching them, listening to them, learning lessons from them that he tries to practice all these years later. To them it probably did not seem like a big deal.

I do not know if he realized what a big deal it was for him to take notice of me. He was the preacher, and I was just a high school senior who decided to make a commitment to Jesus. He encouraged me. He always noticed me and acknowledged my presence. When there were major things going on in my world, he managed to be there with a kind word, a gentle spirit, and usually some amount of money to help me get through college. To him it probably did not seem to be a big deal. To me it was a big deal and his shepherding ministry lives on.

She may not have considered it to be a big deal when she welcomed me into their home as a young man who would eventually marry her daughter. She saw more potential in me than was actually there. She gave me credit for being a better man than I could possibly be. She praised me as a husband and as a father and as a minister and as an important member of the family. To her it was probably not a big deal. To me it has been appreciated for nearly forty years and will be appreciated for the rest of my life.

One time Jesus said these words, *"And if anyone gives even a cup of cold water to one of these little ones who is my disciple, truly I tell you, that person will certainly not lose their reward."* (Matthew 10:42)

As we go through life we will have many opportunities to give *a cup of cold water to one of these little ones*. Let's do everything in our power not to miss those opportunities. Let's notice and acknowledge when someone gives us a cup of cold water. It may not seem like a big deal at the time, but with God's involvement, for some little one it may be a huge deal.

What Is That Aroma?

There sure are a lot of different smells! Odd way to begin an article, right? Seriously, have you ever noticed all the different smells and aromas you encounter every day?

As I leave home in the morning and walk from the bathroom, through the bedroom, through the kitchen, through the laundry room, through the garage, outside, and into my car, each room has a different aroma. From the fresh smell of soap and shampoo and cologne in the bathroom, I pass through the bedroom where the new quilted coverlet has a unique scent. The kitchen smells of brewed coffee and toasted English muffin. The laundry room smells of detergent and hot water. The garage reminds me that it has been raining during the night and the humidity is high. Outside the wet grass and pavement gives off a special and somewhat unpleasant smell. Inside the car I remember that we brought home leftovers from the restaurant last night.

Driving to work the aroma of Starbucks drifts through my window at the drive through. The fragrance of freshly mowed grass seeps through the air vents from the fields on both sides of the road to replace the stifling exhaust from a semi. An occasional stop at the local Donut Palace offers the tempting aroma of freshly baked pastries.

Walking from my car to the office building I notice a neighbor across the street has downed a tree, and the scent of cut wood floats across the parking lot. Inside the door is the familiar smell of the workplace that has no real identifiable source. Passing through the offices the fragrance of fresh flowers or candles is not uncommon.

Further down the hall one detects that meals are being prepared in the kitchen one floor below. Opening the door to my office it is obvious that the door has been closed, and the air has not circulated since Friday afternoon. Turning on the fan and lighting a beach-scented candle restores a freshness to the office.

The variety of odors, aromas, fragrances, and smells on any given day

159

seems to have no limit. The hospital. The grocery store. A restaurant. Coffee shops. Office buildings. People. Each one has its own unique aroma and fragrance. Each uniquely suited for the place or the person. Each one seems to carry a specific image or memory from another place and another time.

It is that imagery that Paul uses to describe what we are to be as followers of Jesus. *But thanks be to God, who always leads us as captives in Christ's triumphal procession and uses us to spread the aroma of the knowledge of him everywhere. For we are to God the pleasing aroma of Christ among those who are being saved and those who are perishing. To the one we are an aroma that brings death; to the other, an aroma that brings life. And who is equal to such a task?* — 2 Corinthians 2:14-16

Just as walking through a house or driving down the street one can experience a variety of pleasant and unpleasant aromas, how we conduct ourselves as we move through the world will produce either a pleasant or unpleasant aroma to those with whom we interact. To our God we are "the pleasing aroma of Christ." What are we to those around us?

Consumed by Weeds

Near the end of the story of the sower (Matthew 7; Mark 4; Luke 8), Jesus makes this statement: *The seed that fell among thorns stands for those who hear, but as they go on their way they are choked by life's worries, riches and pleasures, and they do not mature.* – Luke 8:14

Those words surfaced in my memory recently when I was on a late afternoon walk along the Greenway in what was once a golf course. It's the same golf course I've written about before. It was a beautiful afternoon as I enjoyed the walk with a nice breeze, the setting sun, and listening to a favorite music playlist when I realized I was consumed by weeds.

When I say overcome by weeds I actually mean engulfed by thistles. They have grown tall, almost as tall as me, and have almost completely covered the golf course. As I began to take in the view along the paved path I realized that at eye level and in certain directions all I could see was tall prickly weeds.

That's when I thought of the words of Jesus, ...*they are choked by life's worries, riches and pleasures, and they do not mature.* Those who heard the word were choked by life's worries, riches and pleasures, and they do not mature.

"I know those people," I thought. Then I realized that at times I am one of those people. I am one of those who hear the Word. It makes sense. It is planted into my heart. It begins to grow. Then the weeds appear. They grow. They grow strong and tall and block my vision of the things that are real. Things that are true and clear get choked out by life's worries, riches, pleasures, and they do not mature. I have been there. Maybe you have, too. Maybe you are there now. You are consumed by weeds.

I looked up. Above the weeds. Above the thistles. Further up the path. At the top of the hill. There was a grove of trees. Strong healthy trees. Green lush trees. The weeds had no effect on these trees. They stood firm as if to say, "You can do this. You can survive this. The Word can and will thrive in you."

It was at that moment when I was consumed by the weeds that I realized it was not the trees speaking to me, but the Lord, and I remembered the next verse in Luke 8: *But the seed on good soil stands for those with a noble and good heart, who hear the word, retain it, and by persevering produce a crop.* (Luke 8:15) Consumed by weeds but refreshed by the Word.

Are you consumed by the weeds of life? Look up. Find a tree. Study it. Hear the Lord as He speaks to you and raises you above the weeds.

Living Choices

One of my favorite walking trails takes me through a parcel that was once woods and farm land, then a golf course, and now green space. (I've written other articles about this place.) One of my favorite parts of the trail passes between two ponds. Like other parts of this tract of land that have provided points for reflection and observation since the closure of the golf course, the two ponds remind me of life choices we make on a regular basis: we can choose to survive or we can choose to thrive. (I invite you to listen to "Thrive" by Casting Crowns as you read.)

As I walk I see the pond on the left first. Although there may be good reasons, even healthy reasons, for a pond to be covered with algae like this one, I'm not certain that is the case. I am neither a pond-ologist nor an algae-ologist, but anytime I've ever heard algae being discussed in reference to a pond, pool, or stream, it has been in the context of "How do I kill it or get rid of it?" Never in the context of "Ooooh. Isn't that lovely!" Other than an occasional confused turtle or wandering heron, I rarely see much life in or near this pond. It is as if the pond is in survival mode. Waiting for something to happen to change the course of its existence.

On the other side of the path I see another pond. This one seems to be thriving. Turtles love this pond. They are often seen swimming and sunning on rocks or logs in the pond. Birds of all kinds flit around looking for food. Apparently, fish enjoy this pond, as well, because the bank is often populated by the hopeful fisherman. The water is clear and clean. It seems that a breeze is almost always blowing across this pond.

Again, I do not know the reason for the difference of these two ponds separated by only a short distance (maybe 40-50 feet), and actually connected to some degree by a culvert underneath the road. I do not know the reason, but I see the reality.

So, here is the application. If your life were represented by one of these two ponds, which would it be? Are you just surviving, or are you thriving?

Are you feeling covered up by "stuff"? Do you feel that your very life is being choked out of you by unhealthy influences around you, or in you? Do you feel like you are being overrun by people and events that drain the life out of you? When other people are with you, do they go away drained and discouraged?

Are you feeling alive? Are you living each day in the knowledge that you are God's child and that His Spirit is living in and though you? When people are with you, do they go away feeling refreshed and hopeful?

Consider these two passages from John's Gospel.

The Samaritan woman said to him, "You are a Jew and I am a Samaritan woman. How can you ask me for a drink?" (For Jews do not associate with Samaritans.)

Jesus answered her, "If you knew the gift of God and who it is that asks you for a drink, you would have asked him and he would have given you living water."

"Sir," the woman said, "you have nothing to draw with and the well is deep. Where can you get this living water?" – John 4:9-11

On the last and greatest day of the festival, Jesus stood and said in a loud voice, "Let anyone who is thirsty come to me and drink. Whoever believes in me, as Scripture has said, rivers of living water will flow from within them." By this he meant the Spirit, whom those who believed in him were later to receive. Up to that time the Spirit had not been given, since Jesus had not yet been glorified. – John 7:37-39

We have a choice in how we live. We have a choice in what we offer to others. I pray that this week I will choose in such a way that rivers of living water will flow from within me.

In Her Memory

While Jesus was in Bethany in the home of Simon the Leper, a woman came to him with an alabaster jar of very expensive perfume, which she poured on his head as he was reclining at the table.

When the disciples saw this, they were indignant. "Why this waste?" they asked. "This perfume could have been sold at a high price and the money given to the poor."

Aware of this, Jesus said to them, "Why are you bothering this woman? She has done a beautiful thing to me. The poor you will always have with you, but you will not always have me. When she poured this perfume on my body, she did it to prepare me for burial. Truly I tell you, wherever this gospel is preached throughout the world, what she has done will also be told, in memory of her." – Matthew 26:6-13

There are several lessons we can learn from this story.

There is never a wrong time to approach Jesus. This woman did not care what was going on. She was determined to get to Jesus. She did not care that she was not supposed to interrupt the conversation. She was on a mission to anoint Jesus. She would not be stopped. Jesus did not stop her. Are you feeling the need to move toward Jesus? There is not a wrong time; go to Him.

Some things are more important than money. The disciples were a lot like many of us are in that we allow money and other pragmatic things get in the way of the things that are really important. We de-emphasize expressing emotions and feeling. We call it weakness. Jesus did not consider it weak. His words: *She had done a beautiful thing to me.* Feel like expressing your feelings to Jesus? He welcomes that. Go ahead.

Just because some people think you are foolish does not mean you are foolish. We do not like to be criticized. Too often we withhold our feelings and fail to express our love for the Lord or for another human being because we are afraid of being made fun of, criticized, or rejected. What Jesus thinks about you is more important than what anyone else thinks. If someone tries to stop you, let Him handle them.

Jesus always welcomes a sincere heart. Your words may not eloquent, but He does not care. You may not be able to get through your speech without tears, but that's okay. He can wipe your tears away for you. Your past is ugly, messy, shady, and you feel unacceptable. He is the Master of accepting the ugly, messy, shady, and unacceptable. He looks beyond all that straight into your heart. Is your heart telling you to approach Jesus? He is ready to receive you.

This story needs to be told everywhere. *Wherever the gospel is preached throughout the world, what she has done will also be told, in memory of her.* Tell this story. Better yet, live this story. Be this story. Jesus will welcome you and may tell your story too.

If Everyone Were Like Me

Life would be so much easier for me if everyone were like me.

If everyone were like me, when I tell people I get up early and stay up late to watch the British Open no one would consider me strange.

If everyone were like me, when I tell people I don't like raw tomatoes, no matter how fresh, no one would say, "And you're from the South!"

If everyone were like me, we would all cheer for the Yankees, the Celtics, and the Cowboys.

If everyone were like me, we would never have another heated discussion on politics.

If everyone were like me, wearing jeans, untucked shirts, loafers, and no socks would be the preferred attire for all occasions.

If everyone were like me, mornings would begin slow, easy, quietly and with a really good cup of coffee…just black.

If everyone were like me, Italian food would be on the menu at least once every week…maybe twice.

If everyone were like me, all tables that seat more than two people would be round.

If everyone were like me, it would take about ten seconds for all of us to be bored out of our brains.

Fortunately, not everyone is like me.

In 1 Corinthians 8 Paul gives a very clear illustration that not everyone is like me. He is talking to a group of people who had issues over eating certain kinds of food that emerged from their spiritual heritage. Paul's message here is simple: if I can do or not do something that will enhance your walk with the Lord, I will do it.

In 1 Corinthians 12 Paul describes the Body of Christ like this, *But in fact God has placed the parts in the body, every one of them, just as he wanted them to be. If they were all one part, where would the body be? As it is, there are many parts, but one body.* (1 Corinthians 12:18-19) His message is equally simple: We are all different, and God made us all just the way He wants us.

When I combine the two messages I get this: When I am who God created me to be and you are who God created you to be then we build each other up, we encourage each other to be who we are created to be, our relationships with the Lord will be enhanced, and the Body will be strengthened.

We are all different. God made us different for a reason. He created me to be me, and He created you to be you. I cannot be you, and you cannot be me. I am glad God created us all like we are. I am glad not everyone is like me.

Make Room for Us

2 Corinthians 7 begins with these words: *Make room for us in your hearts.* (v2) Paul is writing to the Christians in Corinth as part of an ongoing relationship with them and in part because of a request for them to give to a special effort to help another group of people. You can read more about that in chapter 8. But for the purposes of this post I want to focus on this one statement: *Make room for us in your hearts.*

Consider the people who are calling out for someone to *Make room for us in your hearts.*

"*Make room for us in your hearts,*" cry the children down the street who need supplies to begin a new school year.

"*Make room for us in your hearts,*" cries the mother who shows up alone at church every Sunday with two small children.

"*Make room for us in your hearts,*" cries the single guy who comes in, sits alone, and quietly leaves alone.

"*Make room for us in your hearts,*" cries the elderly gentleman sitting alone at a table not far from you in the restaurant where you and your church friends go after you leave church services.

"*Make room for us in your hearts,*" cries the line of people standing in the hot sun waiting for their chance to fill a shopping cart with food.

"*Make room for us in your hearts,*" cries the man at the intersection holding a sign that reads: "No job. No home. Will work for food."

"*Make room for us in your hearts,*" cries the child that moves from foster home to foster home.

"*Make room for us in your hearts,*" cries the wife and mother as she feverishly bundles her children in her arms, packs what she can in the car, and escapes to a shelter.

"*Make room for us in your hearts,*" cries the middle-aged man who goes through life alone, a casualty of being on the wrong side of the power systems and still strives to be a blessing to all.

"*Make room for us in your hearts,*" cries the grandparents who have reared their own children and now provide a love-filled home for their grandchildren.

"Make room for us in your hearts," cries the family leaving the comforts of home to move among the people of a distant and poverty-stricken country to remind them that they have made room for them in their hearts.

"Make room for us in your hearts," cries the immigrant coming to America hoping to find a safe place to pursue a life where her gifts and talents are acknowledged, respected, and appreciated.

"Make room for us in your hearts," cries the lonely forgotten masses as they hope for someone somewhere to remember they exist, acknowledge they have value, and believe they are worthy of our attention.

Make room for us in your hearts. Will we hear their cries?

Until Hope Returns

The Story

As soon as the meal was finished, he insisted that the disciples get in the boat and go ahead to the other side while he dismissed the people. When the crowd dispersed, he climbed the mountain so he could be alone and pray. He stayed there alone late into the night.

Meanwhile, the boat was far out to sea when the wind came up against them and they were battered by the waves. At about four o'clock in the morning, Jesus came toward them walking on the water. They were scared to death. "A ghost!" they said, crying out in terror.

But Jesus was quick to comfort them. "Courage, it's me. Don't be afraid."

Peter, suddenly boldly, said, "Master, if it's really you, call me to come to you on the water."

He said, "Come ahead."

Jumping out of the boat, Peter walked on the water to Jesus. But when he looked down at the waves churning beneath his feet, he lost his nerve and started to sink. He cried, "Master, save me!"

Jesus didn't hesitate. He reached down and grabbed his hand. Then he said, "Faint-heart, what got into you?"

The two of them then climbed into the boat, and the wind died down. The disciples in the boat, having watched the whole thing, worshiped Jesus, saying, "This is it! You are God's Son for sure!" – Matthew 14:22-33 (*The Message*)

The Observations

In Mark's and John's accounts, this story immediately follows the story of Jesus feeding five thousand people. Jesus feeds the masses, sends His disciples out in the boat to the other side of the lake, then goes off to be alone. What do you suppose the disciples were thinking?

They surely were amazed, astounded, and more than a little confused by what they had just experienced. According to John (6:15), the crowd was excited and ready to force Jesus to be king. Knowing He needed rest and the crowd needed to settle down, Jesus did what He believed to be

171

best for His disciples. He sends them out in the boat away from the crowd.

They may also have been disappointed. They could sense the momentum building as Jesus traveled through the villages healing, teaching, and gaining followers. Their visions of kingdom, power, and control seemed to be in their grasp, and then Jesus left them to be alone. What is up with that?

In the next scene, the disciples are in a boat in the middle of the night, when Jesus walks toward them. They are terrified until He identifies Himself.

Peter is overcome with excitement and starts walking on the water toward Jesus. Some say the wind scared him. Some say the waves scared him. Some say he took his eyes off Jesus. Some say he suddenly realized what he was doing. Whatever the reason, he started to sink. Jesus pulled him up, and they climbed into the boat.

The Application

As we journey through life, there are times when we are overcome with disappointment and hopelessness, only to be amazed and energized by what happens when we allow God to work within us and among us.

The disciples go from being amazed by the miraculous feeding of the crowd, to being frightened in the boat during a storm, to being overjoyed when Jesus joins them in the boat. Peter probably went from "This is it!" to "This is not it!" to "Hey, look I'm walking on water!" to "Lord save me" to resting safely in the boat.

As you travel through the ups and downs of life, remember this: there will be times when your faith grows weak and your hope begins to fade. When this happens, stay close to Jesus, keep walking with Him, and listen to His voice until hope returns.

The Voices

Some of us are more aware of them than others. The voices, they are always there. I am not talking about strange, psychotic, or disturbing "people would be worried" voices. I am talking about the voices inside of our heads and heart that overpower us and create confusion and anxiety, but at other times calm our spirits and bring us peace and harmony.

Jesus heard the voices.

"You cannot be the Son of God. You are a carpenter's son."

"Jesus, You should demonstrate Your power in such a dramatic way to show people who You really are."

"Jesus, put my sons in positions of leadership in Your kingdom!"

"Jesus, change these stones to bread. Jesus, worship me and I will give You all these kingdoms. Jesus, throw yourself off this high place and prove to me Your loyalty and dedication."

"Jesus, who do You think you are?"

Jesus heard the voices, yet He stayed true to His nature and to His calling.

Thinking about the voices led me to pray this prayer and similar ones many times:

"Father, I hear the voices. They come from all directions. They come from friends who want me to succeed. They come from those who may want to see me fail. Father, help me discern between the voices so that I know when to listen to my head and when to listen to my heart.

"Father, silence the voices that tell me that what I do is insignificant. Silence the voices that tell me I am too good to do this, or that I am not good enough. Silence the voices who speak negativity to my heart.

"Father, increase the volume of the voices that say this is a good thing, you are a good person, you are doing great things, you are touching lives, you are helping people find peace and hope. Increase the volume of the voices that say this is where God wants you, and you are doing what He wants you to do.

"Father, silence the voices that invoke fear. Increase the volume of the voices that instill confidence and trust in You.

"Father, silence the voices that try to tear me down by drawing me away from You. Increase the voices that lift me up and draw me closer to You.

"Father, silence the voices that tell me to be suspicious, skeptical, cynical, and judge those who are different from me. Increase the voices that tell me to be open, to be trusting, and to love all people.

"Father, silence the voices that remind me of my sins and failures. Increase the volume of those voices that remind me of Your forgiveness and the victories that You and I have enjoyed through Your strength.

"The voices are real, Father. Some are good and some are bad. Father, help me discern between the voices and know which ones need to be silenced and which ones need to be heard.

"Father, help me hear Your voice above all others."

I Found the Answer

Be kind and compassionate to one another, forgiving each other, just as in Christ God forgave you. – Ephesians 4:32

I think I found it, the answer to the questions we have been asking ourselves since the beginning of time.

How can I make the world a better place?

What can I do to help stop the violence that is happening around us?

What can I do in my own little circle of influence to make life better for the people closest to me?

The answer isn't profound. It doesn't require a lot of energy, nor will it cost you a cent. It is actually very simple and something we all have the ability to do.

Are you ready to hear what is going to change you and the world around you?

Be kind.

That's it. Just be kind.

Be kind to your spouse, your boyfriend, or girlfriend.

Be kind to your children, your parents, and grandparents.

Be kind to your neighbors, your doctor, and your patients.

Be kind to the cashier at the grocery store, the department store, and the pharmacy.

Be kind to animals, the forests, and our oceans.

Be kind to policemen, firemen, and first responders.

Be kind to the postal worker, the FedEx driver, and even the person who calls to tell you your credit is fine, but…

And most importantly, be kind to yourself. It starts there. It always starts there.

The Day After Easter

Luke ends his account of the life of Jesus like this:

Then he said, "Everything I told you while I was with you comes to this: All the things written about me in the Law of Moses, in the Prophets, and in the Psalms have to be fulfilled."

He went on to open their understanding of the Word of God, showing them how to read their Bibles this way. He said, "You can see now how it is written that the Messiah suffers, rises from the dead on the third day, and then a total life-change through the forgiveness of sins is proclaimed in his name to all nations—starting from here, from Jerusalem! You're the first to hear and see it. You're the witnesses. What comes next is very important: I am sending what my Father promised to you, so stay here in the city until he arrives, until you're equipped with power from on high."

He then led them out of the city over to Bethany. Raising his hands he blessed them, and while blessing them, took his leave, being carried up to heaven.

And they were on their knees, worshiping him. They returned to Jerusalem bursting with joy. They spent all their time in the Temple praising God. Yes. – Luke 24:44-53 (*The Message*)

I hope your Easter Sunday included a time of genuine fellowship, energized and God focused worship, and a message from the Word that challenged you, encouraged you, and inspired you to greater service in the Kingdom of God.

I hope as you spent time over the last week reflecting on the last days of the life of Jesus, you also reflected on how you are living your life, how you would want to spend the last week of your life. I hope now that we have passed through another Easter season you and I will accept the same role as that of those who were with Jesus after His Resurrection. In verse 48 of the text above, Jesus explains their new identity in the Kingdom: *You are the witnesses.*

A witness is one who sees an event. Jesus told them that they have seen the fulfillment of things He had told them would happen. *"You can see now how it is written that the Messiah suffers, rises from the dead on the third day, and then a total life-change through the forgiveness of sins is proclaimed in his name to all nations—starting from here, from Jerusalem! You're the first to hear and see it."* (46-47)

When you are witness, you can testify as to what you have seen. If you see an accident or a crime you may be called into a court of law to serve as a witness, to give a testimony, to confirm or deny what is being said. If you witness something exciting—a great game, a beautiful sunset, or an act of inspirational courage—you cannot wait to share that with others. Given an opening into any conversation, you'll seize it and share what you have seen.

When Jesus tells them, *"You're the witnesses"* He is challenging them and giving them an open door to share what they have seen and experienced. He basically tells them to wait until the Spirit comes to them, but be ready to be the witnesses. If you read further in Luke's writings (the book of Acts), you will see they accept and excel in being His witnesses.

You and I witnessed something yesterday. Because we are witnesses, it is now time for us to share what we saw, what we experienced, how we were impacted, and why it was so significant to us. That is what a witness does. That is what we are.

The only question that remains is will we accept our role as His witnesses?

It is the day after Easter. Will you be His witness?

Do We Really Not Know?

Do We Really Not Know?

We have been going to church all our lives. We have listened to hundreds, maybe thousands of sermons. We have attended conferences, workshops, seminars, and small group studies all designed to help us share our story of faith with other people. We have accumulated all that information and still we act like we do not know what they need.

We have resources at our fingertips that can help us understand our neighbors and give us insight into what life is like outside of the walls of our church buildings. We read books on understanding our times, and we pride ourselves in knowing our communities, and yet we still act like we do not know what the people in our communities need.

We read our Bibles and pray our prayers and sing our songs and offer to help by saying, "If there is anything we can do for you please let us know." We have our times of fellowship, we pat one another on the back, we shake hands and ask, "How are you doing?" and sometimes they tell us. We know people are hurting, and we know they are in need, and yet we act like we do not know what they need.

Obviously, these scenarios are not always true. Not all churches and not all Christians act like we do not know what people need, but many do. Do we really not know?

Do we really not know that marriages that are in trouble need help learning better and more effective ways to communicate and become better at managing their money or solid Biblical teaching about being married?

Do we really not know that parents who are having trouble with their teenage son or daughter need help understanding what life is like for a teenager, knowing how to communicate with their teen, and learning what it means to be a parent?

Do we really not know that the family of a fifteen-year-old boy who was shot in his own driveway needs help dealing with the shock, anger, and pure sadness that comes with such a loss?

Do we really not know that the family of the eleven-year-old boy responsible for the shooting need help as they deal with the confusion, the guilt, and the loss of their son being taken from them?

Do we really not know that the woman who lost her husband after fifty years of marriage needs help to move through the grieving process?

Do we really not know that a teenage girl dealing with all the pressures of being a teenage girl needs a mother, or a grandmother, or another godly woman to invite her into life where a relationship of trust and understanding can grow?

Do we really not know? As followers of Jesus, after reading of His life, after knowing how He lived and loved and served and touched people, do we really not know? Maybe if we remember what He came to do it might help us remember.

Jesus returned to Galilee in the power of the Spirit, and news about him spread through the whole countryside. He was teaching in their synagogues, and everyone praised him.

He went to Nazareth, where he had been brought up, and on the Sabbath day he went into the synagogue, as was his custom. He stood up to read, and the scroll of the prophet Isaiah was handed to him. Unrolling it, he found the place where it is written:

"The Spirit of the Lord is on me, because he has anointed me to proclaim good news to the poor. He has sent me to proclaim freedom for the prisoners and recovery of sight for the blind, to set the oppressed free, to proclaim the year of the Lord's favor."

Then he rolled up the scroll, gave it back to the attendant and sat down. The eyes of everyone in the synagogue were fastened on him. He began by saying to them, "Today this scripture is fulfilled in your hearing." – Luke 4:14-23

Do we really not know?

Be Creative with Encouragement

After I had completed my comments, I moved back to my seat as others continued participation in the time of communion. Just as I was about to sit down a young woman whom I had never met moved up beside me and introduced herself. She had been present a time or two before but we had never talked.

She proceeded to tell me how she felt compelled by God to talk to me. I assumed she was struggling with something and needed prayer or guidance. I was stunned to learn that she was simply seizing the moment to encourage me. She was not needing me to tell her "everything will be all right," to offer words of hope for her, nor did she need me to pray for her. Instead, she wanted to encourage me.

She spoke of how she felt the presence of God in me as I spoke. She sincerely explained that she genuinely felt that God was using me to make a difference in this church and that she was deeply grateful for me letting Him guide me as I serve in His Kingdom.

That's it. She encouraged me and then moved back to her seat.

I learned later that she had shared similar words with another of our members. Both of us expressed how we were moved to tears.

Earlier in the service our youth minister shared this passage:

Therefore, brothers, since we have confidence to enter the Most Holy Place by the blood of Jesus, by a new and living way opened for us through the curtain, that is, his body, and since we have a great priest over the house of God, let us draw near to God with a sincere heart in full assurance of faith, having our hearts sprinkled to cleanse us from a guilty conscience and having our bodies washed with pure water. Let us hold unswervingly to the hope we profess, for he who promised is faithful. And let us consider how we may spur one another on toward love and good deeds. Let us not give up meeting together, as some are in the habit of doing, but let us encourage one another—and all the more as you see the Day approaching. – Hebrews 10:19–25 (NIV84)

This kind and attentive woman obviously took God at His word and considered how she might *spur another on toward love and good deeds*.

Let's see how inventive we can be in encouraging love and helping out... - Hebrews 10:24 (*The Message*)

She had considered, she pondered, she thought about how she might encourage me. Then she did it.

She sought me out of the crowd. She took the risk of interrupting me from my private thoughts about the Lord's sacrifice and encouraged me.

She took advantage of the opportunity to share a kind and genuine message of encouragement with the one who sees it as his role to encourage others.

She was creative. She was brave. She could have waited until the end of the service. She could have written me a note, or a text, or an email. She could have messaged me on *Facebook*. She did none of these. Instead she took advantage of a moment to tell me face to face that she sensed God's presence in me.

I felt guilty for assuming she was a needy person coming to ask me for help. I felt ashamed of my arrogance. I felt sad that I had labeled her as a taker. I felt all that, but mostly I felt blessed that she was a giver, a noticer, and an encourager. I felt honored that she had taken the time to seek me out and share the message God had placed on her heart.

I was blessed that morning. I will continue to be blessed every time I think about her. I will be challenged by her example to seek out someone to encourage, someone to bless, or someone to express my appreciation for how they are allowing God to be visible in and through them.

Let's see how inventive and creative we can be in encouraging others to love and do good deeds. Let's consider it, and let's do it.

It Doesn't Take Long

There is a golf course, or I should say, there *was* a golf course in our community. The course was once a fairly popular private golf course and country club which included a club house, swimming pool, and tennis courts. The course closed at the end of last year.

Although the decision to close the course had been made more than a year before the actual closing, the maintenance workers had done a good job of taking care of the course right up to the closing. Fairways were mowed. Greens were cared for. Sand traps never were great, but they tried to take care of them. That was then. That was less than six months ago.

To see the course now one has to remind oneself that six months ago it was a functioning golf course. The hard, lingering winter, heavy spring rains, and lack of care has transformed the course into an abandoned forgotten tract of land that may someday be turned into a park or green space. The downward transformation did not take long.

In a matter of months, fairways have been covered with weeds, great clusters of clover, and wind-blown trees. Fallen limbs and trees that once would have been cleaned up have been left along cart paths and the edges of fairways. Greens are now filled with weeds and gopher trails. Carl Spackler, where are you?

For a golfer who enjoyed an occasional round on the old course and taking photographs of the beautiful colors of fall, this is a sad sight. But there are other things that can take a downward turn quickly when the proper care and attention are discontinued.

When a couple fails to give their marriage appropriate time and attention, the relationship can begin to suffer quickly.

When one stops giving attention to his physical condition — stops eating healthy foods, stops exercising, stops getting proper rest — his body will suffer, and serious health problems can develop.

When parents fail to give their children the love and protection and security they need, the development of the child can be disrupted and delayed.

When an employee fails to give his or her job the attention it needs, not only can his or her position with the company be jeopardized, but the company itself can be affected.

When leaders of a church fail to give the love and care that the people under their care need and deserve, the whole body will suffer.

When one fails to feed his soul with spiritual food and receive the nourishment of a healthy spiritual family, he will grow weak and vulnerable and become easy prey for attacks from the Enemy.

This passage from the New Testament book of Hebrews emphasizes the importance of providing care and encouragement for one another:

See to it, brothers and sisters, that none of you has a sinful, unbelieving heart that turns away from the living God. But encourage one another daily, as long as it is called "Today," so that none of you may be hardened by sin's deceitfulness. We have come to share in Christ, if indeed we hold our original conviction firmly to the very end. – Hebrews 3:12-14

Now the questions: Are you taking care of yourself? Are you feeding your soul? Are you nurturing your relationships? Are you fulfilling your role as a fellow believer? If you are, good! Please continue and look for more opportunities to increase your efforts. If you are not, please consider this a warning from someone who cares for your soul — even though I may not know you — I care. You need to take care of yourself and your relationships – especially your relationship with the Lord. It doesn't take long to see the negative consequences.

Please start today. Please do not stop. Please look around at those you love, and if they need your help, your support, your love, or your encouragement, give it. If you need these same things from them, ask for them.

It doesn't take long.

Your Act of Worship

Therefore, I urge you, brothers and sisters, in view of God's mercy, to offer your bodies as a living sacrifice, holy and pleasing to God — this is your true and proper worship. – Romans 12:1

And so, dear brothers and sisters, I plead with you to give your bodies to God because of all he has done for you. Let them be a living and holy sacrifice—the kind he will find acceptable. This is truly the way to worship him. – Romans 12:1 (*New Living Translation*)

Therefore I urge you, brethren, by the mercies of God, to present your bodies a living and holy sacrifice, acceptable to God, which is your spiritual service of worship. – Romans 12:1 (*New American Standard*)

So here's what I want you to do, God helping you: Take your everyday, ordinary life — your sleeping, eating, going-to-work, and walking-around life — and place it before God as an offering. Embracing what God does for you is the best thing you can do for him. – Romans 12:1 (*The Message*)

I beseech you therefore, brethren, by the mercies of God, that ye present your bodies a living sacrifice, holy, acceptable unto God, which is your reasonable service. – Romans 12:1 (*King James Version*)

I shared these five different versions of this verse (and I consulted several others) because I was looking for the translation, paraphrase, or version that says that our worship only happens on Sunday morning in a pew inside a church building. I know it has to be there, I have heard it all my life. But where does it say that? Oh, well.

If I understand this passage, worship happens when I give myself to God. If that is the case and if I have given myself to God, then it seems logical that my entire life is worship. I suppose that's why Eugene Peterson (*The Message*) translated, *Take your everyday, ordinary life—your sleeping, eating, going-to-work, and walking-around life—and place it before God as an offering.*

What does that mean? That means…

When you are at your job, driving to your job, or listening to a coworker share their pain about their struggling marriage, you are worshipping.

When you are putting your children to bed, fixing them breakfast, driving them to school, changing a diaper, or kissing a boo-boo, you are worshipping.

When you are playing softball, coaching little league, or sitting in the parking lot waiting for practice to end, you are worshipping.

When you are teaching algebra, repairing a carburetor, or preparing a meal for a sick friend, you are worshipping.

When helping your mom carry in the groceries, babysitting your little brother, or walking your dog, you are worshipping.

When you are sitting alone on the beach, hiking a mountain trail, or watching a sunset, you are worshipping.

Take your everyday, ordinary life — your sleeping, eating, going-to-work, and walking-around life, and enjoy your life of wholehearted worship to God.

When You Understand

You never know what lies behind the actions, words, or attitude of another human being unless somehow you are able to connect with them in a real and meaningful way. When we do not know, we assume, we judge, and we condemn. This story from Brennan Manning's *Abba's Child* illustrates it powerfully:

> "Understanding triggers the compassion that makes forgiveness possible. Author Stephen Covey recalled an incident while riding the New York City subway one Sunday morning. The few passengers aboard were reading the newspaper or dozing. It was a quiet, almost somnolent ride through the bowels of the Big Apple. Covey was engrossed in reading when a man accompanied by several small children boarded at the next stop. In less than a minute, bedlam erupted. The kids ran up and down the aisle shouting, screaming, and wrestling with one another on the floor. Their father made no attempt to intervene.
>
> The elderly passengers shifted nervously. Stress became distress. Covey waited patiently. Surely the father would do something to restore order: a gentle word of correction, a stern command, some expression of paternal authority—anything. None was forthcoming. Frustration mounted.
>
> After an unduly generous pause, Covey turned to the father and said kindly, 'Sir, perhaps you could restore order here by telling your children to come back and sit down.'
>
> 'I know I should do something,' the man replied. 'We just came from the hospital. Their mother died an hour ago. I just don't know what to do.'" (Excerpt From: Manning, Brennan. *Abba's Child*. NavPress, 2002. iBooks.)

Manning concludes the section with this statement: "The heartfelt compassion that hastens forgiveness matures when we discover where our enemy cries."

Anything like that ever happen to you? A child is misbehaving, a teenager wearing baggy jeans that look like they might drop to the floor any second, the couple at the table next to you having an intense conversation that makes you and most of the other people in the restaurant uncomfortable, the clerk snaps at you when you ask a simple question, your spouse seems distant and irritable, or your child storms the table after spewing words that cut you to the core of your soul and breaks your heart.

Be very thoughtful with your next move. The life of the relationship depends on how you choose to respond.

You can assume the worst. "He's such a jerk!" "She is so hateful!"

You can respond in kind. "You treat me like that, and you'll be sorry." "Forget you!"

You can react with even worse words. "You good-for-nothing lazy bum!"

There is another option.

When you are confronted with a person or a situation where your immediate and natural reaction or response is to judge, be critical, or assume the absolute worst about the person, stop. Stop right there and consider that there is more to the story than you can possibly see. In time, you may be able to build a relationship with the person and learn the pain behind the defensive and non-trusting attitude. The guy did not start out like he is now. The woman did not plan for her life to be as painful as it is. The teenager did not wake up one morning saying, "I am going be as mean and selfish and hard to get along with as I can possibly be for the rest of my life." Something happened.

As a follower of Jesus, we do a great service when we take time to ask a few questions, not make assumptions, and move in as close as we can get to the person and listen to their story. It may take time (it usually does) to get close enough and show them that you can be trusted with their pain. It may never happen in some cases where the pain is so deep and so great. But you will be transformed when you take the time, make the effort, and allow God to open your eyes to really see inside the person.

Something to keep in mind: Sometimes even when you know the back story, the guy *is* a jerk, she really *is* that hateful, and that couple actually *is* trying to manipulate you. That may be true. You cannot change who they are or the circumstances that made them the way they are. But you can change how you think, feel, and respond to them. Some will not allow you inside their protective cover, but don't stop hoping they will. If you push too hard, they will run.

I am reminded of the people Jesus met who had been rejected by society. The woman at the well (John 4), the woman caught in adultery (John 8), the blind man (John 9), and others. Instead of joining the crowd and saying, "You are worthless!" Jesus responded with gentle, loving words. Jesus started with forgiving eyes and tender touches. Jesus started by trying to understand the reason behind their cries.

You can do that, too. You have His Spirit living in you. You have the opportunities to disarm an angry, hurting, and broken man or woman or child or teenager who knows only pain, disappointment, and anger. You may be the one person God has placed in that person's path to show them a different way. They may be the one person God has placed in your path to show you a different way.

Lead with love and compassion. Jesus did that with you. Look what that has done in your life.

Part Three

Hoping

The life of Jesus and His followers is a life filled with hope. Not a life without challenge, struggle, pain and suffering, but a life of hope in spite of those things. Because of our hope in Jesus we know that failure, disappointment, and death are not the end but the true beginning of life. The grave is not the end. Pain is not eternal. Our hope is in Jesus the risen Lord.

Very truly I tell you, unless a kernel of wheat falls to the ground and dies, it remains only a single seed. But if it dies, it produces many seeds.
John 12:24

My prayer is that as you pass through all of the challenges life brings your way you will find hope in Jesus, the living hope.

The Next Thing

Not long ago my two brothers and I were visiting in a chat room. Our discussion was the typical light-hearted banter that has caused some people to affectionately describe us "clowns," or perhaps more appropriately: The Three Stooges. Suddenly the tone changed with a serious question about handling life's decisions, life's disappointments, and remaining faithful and confident in spite of life's sometimes confusing events. After the question, there was another period of joking and a few not-so-serious suggestions until my oldest brother shared a concept from Elizabeth Elliot on dealing with grief. She described a lady who after the death of her husband, went into her house, got the broom, and started to sweep the floor. When asked how she survived the sudden, premature, and tragic death of her husband, the woman answered, "I just began to do the next thing there was to do."

Do the next thing. Needless to say, this bit of counsel launched us into a whole new realm which has spilled over into other conversations. My initial reaction to the suggestion was, "How do you know what the next thing is?" Then I added, "Sometimes my struggle is – once I know what the next thing is, I don't want to do that next thing. I want a different next thing." After a few more comments, the Norvell trio pretty much agreed that whether we like it or not, and whether we want to do it or not, doing the next thing is good advice, and explains how we have been able to survive of our own set-backs and wilderness wanderings. We just do the next thing.

When you think about it, it makes sense. When tragedy occurs (a death, a serious accident, a great disappointment, a dream dies), sometimes the best thing you can do is to do the next thing. You don't have to think a lot about it. You usually don't have to sit and ponder it very long. You simply do the next thing.

The New Testament has several examples of doing the next thing.

In John 11, when Jesus received word that his dear friend Lazarus was deathly sick, He did the next thing. *He stayed where he was two more days* (John 11:6). Then when He arrived in Bethany and learned that Lazarus had died, He brought him back to life. He was filled with grief, but He did the next thing.

When Jesus learned that the way of the cross was the only way to please the Father, He did the next thing – He went to the cross.

After Jesus had died on the cross, His disciples were scattered, broken, disappointed, and confused. But they did the next thing. Joseph took the body to the tomb. The two women later went to the tomb. Discovering the empty tomb, they ran to tell the others.

When Jesus confronted guilt-ridden and embarrassed Peter after the resurrection, He instructed him to do the next thing – *feed my sheep* (John 21). Peter did the next thing. He fed the sheep.

When the disciples, filled with the Holy Spirit, began spreading the message of Good News throughout the world, they were met with opposition, but they did the next thing. They continued to speak. When told they must stop speaking about Jesus, they spoke to one more person.

When Paul's dreams of going to Rome to preach to the masses turned into being confined to his prison-home, he did the next thing. He wrote letters. Letters that remind us to do the next thing.

When those who followed God were met with opposition, difficulty, suffering, loss, or disappointment, they did the next thing.

Now, it is your turn.

Your life has not turned out anything at all like you planned. You feel like a failure in some ways. You are disheartened. You are discouraged. You are frustrated. You would like to quit. Instead, may I suggest you do the next thing.

You were almost there. You were so close to the promotion you could see your name going up on the door. But your boss changed his mind. You are not going anywhere. You are staying right where you are. What should you do? Do the next thing.

Without warning your husband has announced that he is "tired of this life" and wants out. You try, but his decision is final. He leaves. What are you supposed to do? Do the next thing.

The call in the middle of the night informs you that your mother has had a stroke. Within a few days you realize that someone has to take care of her. You are filled with questions that have no easy answers. What are you going to do? Do the next thing.

You have been healthy for all your life, but suddenly you find yourself sitting next to your husband in the doctor's office when you think you heard the doctor say something about cancer. Is it true? Is this really happening to me? Is it really cancer? What are you going to do? Do the next thing.

Your daughter wakes you in the middle of the night with the words, "I need to talk to you." Within minutes your entire world has changed with the news: "I'm pregnant." She is only sixteen. What in the world are you going to do? What can you do to help her? Do the next thing.

You hugged your son and told him you loved him. The next thing you know you are listening to a stranger's voice on the other end of a telephone conversation telling you your son was killed in a car accident. No one's fault. No one to blame. It was a freak accident. How will you go on? What can you do? How will you survive this? Do the next thing.

You have worked for the same company for thirty years. You have done a good job. You felt secure. You came to work as usual. There on your desk was the memo informing you that the company had been sold. You see the word: downsizing. Your position has been eliminated. You feel as though you have been eliminated. You are out of a job. What will you do? You will do the next thing.

It is easy to sit at my computer and tell you to do the next thing. Obviously, doing it is not always easy, nor is it always crystal clear what the next thing to be done actually is. The next thing for one person is not the same thing as the next thing for someone else. First, pray (that may be the next thing) for strength and wisdom to discover the next thing. Then once you figure it out, do the next thing. Don't try to do the next ten things, or the next five things, or the next three things, or even the next two things, just do the next thing. Then after that, do the next thing, do the next thing. Doing the next thing will not only help you survive whatever you are going through, doing the next thing will help you live again. Doing the next thing may be the one thing that will help you get through the days ahead. So, even if the next thing is not the thing you had in mind to do, go ahead – do the next thing.

Enjoy the next thing.

More Than Just a Flower

I cannot remember a year when I looked forward to spring as much as this year. Our winter would probably be considered wimpy by some standards, but the one big snow storm, the other less severe ones, an ice storm, the lingering piles of dirty snow along the sides of the road and in parking lots, plus the bare trees, brown grass, and gray skies were almost too much even for this snow-loving-cold-weather-fan. I was ready for a change.

That is why that first yellow bloom was such a welcome site. A single jonquil, in the yard of a vacant house with a parched lawn for a background, stood all alone delivering a message of hope.

Sometimes we need a reminder that better days are ahead, that things are going to change, that our load will be lightened. Hope may first show itself as a flower, a letter, a phone call, or a visit. Regardless of its appearance, there are times when a sign of hope is what we need to keep holding on.

For the homeless, hope may be ignited when a family invites them to share a meal in their home, offers friendship, or demonstrates genuine love.

For the worker in the same "going-no-where" job for too many years, hope may bloom as an invitation to the boss' office to discuss a future with the company.

For the mother buried under piles of laundry, stacks of dishes, and rooms of toys, hope may present itself when her husband says, "I'm sorry I have not been more helpful. I'm going to do better."

For the couple behind with their bills, hope may show up when they open their mail and find a check from a beloved aunt.

For the oppressed, mistreated, and forgotten, hope came as a baby boy named Jesus. Later hope appeared as a boy answering and asking questions in the temple. Amazingly hope was found hanging on a cross. Ultimately, hope was revealed as an empty tomb. Today, hope exists in the image of a cross.

If you have grown weary of the dark clouds filling your world, don't give up. Spring is coming. Keep looking. There are little yellow flowers popping up everywhere just waiting to remind you of the hope that exists in Him.

Enjoy the flower.

Going on Alone

I met a man last week just a few hours after he had lost his wife of sixty-two years. He apologized for being selfish for wanting her to stay, yet he also said he knew she was better off. Tears rolled from his eyes as one of our shepherds worded a sweet prayer of comfort for him and his family as he faced the reality that he must go on alone.

I have thought about this gentleman almost constantly since that meeting. I have pondered and tried to imagine what it would be like to say goodbye to a companion of sixty-two years. How do you let go? How is he supposed to go on? What is he supposed to do? What is he supposed to think when he gets up in the morning and is forced to realize that the woman he has loved since they both were young is no longer with him? What can anyone say to him that can ease the pain of going on alone?

I don't know if I have any great words of wisdom for anyone who has just lost a mate, a mate of sixty-two years, or a mate of only a short time, but there are some things that I have learned from observing couples that have lived long and loved strong.

First, try to live in such a way that there are no regrets. Take advantage of every opportunity you have to be together and every opportunity to strengthen your marriage. Regardless of the length of your marriage, make sure it is full, rich, and alive.

Second, never miss an opportunity to express your love. This is true in any relationship. There is an ache unlike any other ache when you long to say "I love you," and the object of your love is either no longer there to hear the words or is in such a condition that you don't know if they can hear your words, simple words that we feel in the depths of our souls, but too often fail to verbalize. Sure, actions may speak louder than words, but the words also speak.

Third, when the end comes, and you are reminded of your vows, "Until death do us part," go on from that day with courage and confidence that God is going with you. I know it is not the one person on this earth who means more to you than all the rest of creation, but it is the One that created all those things. Walk with Him. Talk with Him. Let Him bring you comfort and provide the strength you need to go on alone. He is the only one that can help us do that.

This will be a tough week for many people. This gentleman I mentioned has lost his Valentine. This will the first time others have walked through the card section of the store and realized there is no need to stop. Others are longing for that special person they hope is out there somewhere but have never found. The best I can offer, and I know it sounds a bit hollow, is to continue to walk with the Lord. If you know someone who is going on alone, reach out to them, share your love with them, put your arms around them, say the words they long to hear as they go on alone.

Enjoy those you love.

One Hour

One hour I received a phone call from a friend telling of the birth of a healthy baby boy. The next hour I talked with a man who fears his only son has lost his way and may never find his way home.

One hour the late evening news reminds me that another warning of a possible terrorist attack has been issued. An hour later my favorite team comes from behind to win a game in the World Series (update: the other team just came back to win the series).

One hour I am laughing as a friend shares a story about her happy childhood. An hour or so later I am handing a box of tissues to a lady as she tells her story of a very unhappy and tragic childhood.

One hour I am reading of God's goodness and kindness and saying my prayers. An hour later I am sitting in traffic thinking very unkind thoughts about the person in front of me.

One hour life is simple and uncomplicated. An hour later I realize that life has changed completely and has become very complicated.

One hour I'm leading a discussion of how marriages get into trouble and how families fall apart. An hour later I'm watching families demonstrate how to make good marriages better and how strong families can grow stronger.

One hour I'm watching the sunrise and marveling at God's creation. An hour later I see only clouds and question His actions.

Unless I miss my guess, some who read these words have experienced (are experiencing) these same shifts in attitude, disposition, and life perspective. That is life, isn't it? Up and down. High and low. Good and bad. Happiness and sorrow. Joy and pain. Success and failure. Life has always been that way.

One hour Adam and Eve were enjoying God's special garden, the next hour they were driven from that garden. One hour God's people were faithful and true, the next they were rebellious and selfish. One hour David was a powerful king, the next he was tempted and weak. One hour the followers of Jesus felt betrayed and bewildered by seeing Jesus dying on a cross, the next they were overjoyed and courageously sharing the story of their risen Lord.

One hour can make a lot of difference. Stay with it!

Disappointment Turns to Joy

Like most children in our area I was disappointed when I awoke to realize that the predictions of two to four inches of snow were not going to happen. Every weather forecaster in our area agreed, "We will get snow!" Apprehensive, but hopeful, I went to bed expecting to see the ground covered by the white stuff the next morning. Instead, we had rain. A little snow. But a far cry from two to four inches. No accumulation. No cancellations. No snow men. Not even a snow ball fight.

Being disappointed because it did not snow is one thing. I have learned (or hope I am learning) to deal with it. By the end of the day I am usually fine. However, other disappointments are not so easy to handle.

Your team has been winning all season. They have a real chance to win the championship. They only need to win one more game. As the clock ticks down toward the end of the game your team has the lead. Then at the last second the other team scores. It's over.

You've been sick of your job for years. You think you are finally getting your chance. You've prayed for the opportunity. You're confident. Then you get the call, "You didn't get the job."

You've dealt with the disease. You've followed the doctor's orders. You've rested. You've taken your medicine. You've prayed. But then you hear the doctor say, "It's back."

You've prayed all your life for a Godly mate. You think you have found her. The relationship is progressing nicely. Then out of the blue, she tells you, "It's over."

Your hopes are gone. Your dreams have faded. What might have been, will not be. What do you do? How do you deal with the disappointment?

When those following Jesus faced their great disappointment and saw their dreams dying on the cross, they were confused. They waited. They hoped. They prayed. They listened. They opened their eyes. They opened their hearts. They saw Jesus. They believed. Their disappointment turned to joy.

I cannot promise that if you follow these steps you'll wake up tomorrow and find your neighborhood covered in snow. But if you deal with your disappointments the way these disciples did, I do promise that your disappointment will eventually turn to joy. Don't let disappointment defeat you.

Keep hope in your heart.

A Spring Surprise

Those who have been reading for a while may remember that last fall I planted flowers in our yard, my first experience at trying to get something to grow. I dug the holes, placed the bulbs in the holes, covered the holes with potting soil, watered them, and basically left them alone. As the temperatures of fall and winter continued to drop I wondered if they would survive. Quite frankly, I was not real optimistic about my ability as a gardener.

As winter passed and the warm sunshine of early spring arrived, I became increasingly more interested in what might appear. One day there were stems poking through the dirt. They grew taller and taller. Then there were blooms that appeared waiting to open. Suddenly they began to open. There were real tulips blooming in our yard. Red tulips. Orange (actually sort of soft peach color) tulips. I even have a few purple tulips (unless last night's freeze killed them). I have been ecstatic with the flowers that have bloomed.

But there was some disappointment in that there were only tulips. You see I had also planted daffodils. They are my favorite. Since I did not remember where I planted what particular flower, I really didn't know where to look. But I did know that I was not seeing daffodils anywhere, and that made me sad. Then one day last week an amazing thing happened. Those things that had sprung up in a circle around my mailbox turned out to be daffodils. Huge daffodils. Bright solid yellow daffodils and yellow and white daffodils. I was thrilled! I'm still thrilled.

Why am I so excited about flowers? Some may have their own answer for that question, but here's mine: I am thrilled that the seed I planted produced fruit. Bulbs became flowers. I was not sure I would ever see any real results from my days in the soil. I'm not taking credit for it. All I did was plant the seed remember. God watered. God provided the sunshine. God put the proper nutrients in the soil. God produced the flowers. But I helped. I planted the seed.

Not long ago I received an email from a young lady that we had known when she was a college student. My wife and I loved here. We encouraged her. I even had the privilege of baptizing her. We had not heard from her in over twenty years. Somehow she came across one of my articles and sent me a note telling me of her life. Though there has been some sadness, she is still serving the Lord and raising children to serve the Lord. As I read the email, I realized that seed we were able to plant in her heart has taken root and is now producing beautiful fruit for God. All we did was plant some seed. God did the rest.

I am able to enjoy flowers in our yard because I planted the seed. I am enjoying a kind of joy in life today because of fruit that is being produced from seed that was planted years ago. Some who are reading this note will, I hope, see these words as flowers that are blooming because of the seed that you planted in my heart decades ago. Thank you for having faith to plant the seed. Thank you for showing me the value in planting seed.

I tell you the truth, unless a kernel of wheat falls to the ground and dies, it remains only a single seed. But if it dies, it produces many seed. – John 12:24

Keep planting those seeds. God has a surprise in store for you.

Just A Glimpse

Driving around the city as the trees display their fall colors, I occasionally find myself wanting to pause and gaze at the brilliant colors. I would like to stop my car in the middle of the road for just a moment to enjoy the leaves as they gently float to the ground. Something inside me reminds me that if I don't stop now, they will be gone tomorrow. Leaves do not last long in the rain and wind. I feel a sense of urgency about stopping, but I do not. Schedules, people traveling behind me, police officers do not allow it. So, I settle for just a glimpse of God's beauty.

A similar feeling comes over me when I look at my children. They change so quickly. They grow so fast. In what seems like only a moment they go from being a little boy who wants to play ball, to a grown man wanting to get on with his life. In a blink of an eye she moved from a curly haired little girl from her swing saying, "Push me, Daddy!" to a developing young lady saying, "Don't push me, Dad. I'll be all right." There are times I'd like to slow things down and enjoy the view for a little longer, but life moves on and I must settle for just a glimpse as they pass through my view.

There are times when I feel so close to God that I would like to stop the clock and stay in that setting. The sense of peace and the power of His presence is so comforting. I cannot imagine anything any better. But that time ends. The retreat ends. The walk is over. The assembly disperses. Life interrupts. The peace is replaced with commotion. The tranquility is pushed aside by chaos. So, I settle for just a glimpse of what Heaven will be like.

There are times when I feel like I have finally figured out what this God-pleasing life is all about. I am thinking the right things, I am doing the right things, I am becoming the right kind of person. I begin to think that I am actually beginning to allow others to see Jesus living in me. Then I blow it. I go back to my old ways, my old systems, my old devices. It was nice while it lasted, but I settle for just a glimpse of what it is means to live like Jesus.

There are many images that pass through our sight that are only there for a brief moment. If we fail to take them in they will be gone forever. Relationships. Opportunities. Experiences. All are there for our enjoyment and pleasure. Don't settle for just a glimpse. Take time. Linger a little longer. Drink deeply. Be thankful. Enjoy.

This week as you gather with your family and friends over a Thanksgiving dinner, take time to enjoy it completely. Don't hurry through this holiday. Don't settle for just a glimpse of what it could be.

The next time you notice a beautiful tree by the side of the road with the leaves swirling in the wind, check to make sure no one is behind you, then pull off the side of the road, and watch the leaves fall. Don't settle for just a glimpse.

Enjoy this season completely.

The Folded Page

As I opened my Bible to the section of Scripture I had been reading before the interruption, I noticed that I had carelessly allowed the page to get folded leaving a huge wrinkle in the page. Not a small corner fold, but an ugly uneven fold in two or three places. That page would never be the same. No matter how many times I try to close my Bible and press the wrinkle out of sight, when I open it to that page, the reminder of my carelessness will be there.

Many would pass this off as no big deal. Maybe I should as well, but for this self-admitting neat nick the wrinkled page has become a painful reminder of the impact sin has in our lives. Even the sins we might label as "small sins" have a way of staying with us.

She is married and has grown children of her own, but every time she looks in the mirror she sees something no one else ever sees. She sees the scar. The scar she keeps covered with make-up. Each time she sees the scar she relives the pain of her father's drunken rage when she was a little girl.

He is in his fifties and by most accounts would be considered a success. He has a good job. He is respected by many in the community. However, in his own mind it is never good enough. He can never work enough hours. His check is never fat enough. He cannot climb the ladder fast enough. Not matter how hard he tries, he cannot erase the words spoken so long ago: "You will never amount to anything!"

They have been married for thirty years and are seen by others as the ideal couple. They do have a good marriage. They have worked hard to forgive and forget. Still there are times when that one event enters the conversation and tempers flare, hurtful words are spoken, and a little of the joy seeps out of their relationship.

The doctor tries to comfort the family as he explains, "We did everything possible for your daughter." Those words do little to ease the suffering of this mother and father as they must come to terms with the results of her one foolish attempt to be part of the crowd.

The page in my Bible will probably never be the same. It will always remind me of my carelessness. I can live with the wrinkled page. For these deeper wrinkles – these scars of our heart – that are there because of sins we have committed, because of sins committed against us, or because of the thoughtless acts of those we love are difficult to live with. For these we need more. We need the reminder of God's concern for our pain: *The Lord is close to the brokenhearted* – Psalm 34:18

We need a refresher on being renewed in our walk with God (Psalm 51).

We need the assurance of knowing that we have a very forgiving God (1 John 1:5-10).

I really do not have a solution for those pages in your Bible that have accidentally gotten folded and wrinkled. I do have a solution for the heart that is broken and scarred. Jesus. The Savior of the world. The forgiver of our sins. Give Him your broken heart. Let Him straighten out the wrinkles. Allow Him to heal your hurts.

He can handle all your folded pages.

9-11-02 Fears and Hopes

As the first anniversary of the tragic events of 9/11/01 is upon us, I find myself (probably like many of you) reflecting on the last year and how it has impacted and affected myself, our nation, and the world. Or if it has. I've narrowed my reflections down to two categories: Fears and Hopes.

My fears include:

I fear that nothing has changed. Some of the materials I read indicate that shortly after the events of 9/11/01 the interests in spiritual things increased significantly. Prayer was more common. Using God's name properly was more important. Discussion of the topic of God's providential care for His people was very common. Now, a year later, it seems that much of that has subsided. I fear that it is possible for us to experience true change as a people and less than a year later have only surface expressions.

I fear that we have changed too much. The events of 9/11/01 caused some to turn to God in loving trust and caused others to turn away from Him in anger and rage. Some have come away from 9/11/01 afraid to live, afraid to trust, afraid to travel, afraid to hope. Some have developed a deeper patriotic spirit; others have deepened their commitment to an anti-patriotic spirit. I fear we have changed too much.

I fear that some are more convinced than ever that being different is bad. The way one looks, the color of the skin, the way one dresses, even the language that is spoken is not what makes one good or bad. What makes one good or bad depends on what is in and what comes out of the heart. As a result of 9/11/01, some now perceive anyone who is "not like us" to be against us. The opposite is also concerning; just because someone looks like us and talks like us does not indicate the condition of the heart.

I fear that we will adopt a belief that power makes right. Political power. Economic power. Intellectual power. Physical power. Might makes right. If my weapons are bigger than your weapons, and if my armies can defeat your armies, that is proof that I am right. In the search for physical supremacy I fear we will lose sight of where our true source of power comes from.

I fear that because of what happened or did not happen on 9/11/01 many are doubting the presence of God in the world. God was present in the Towers, in the planes, in the Pentagon, on the ground, in the streets, in the homes, and in the hearts of everyone who suffered and or died on 9/11/01. His presence did not prevent what happened, nor did it cause it. But He was there. He is still available for all who choose to allow Him to rule their hearts. I fear that we will not doubt that.

My hopes include:

I hope that we are more aware of God's presence in our lives. At least, I hope we are more aware of the need for God's presence in our lives. Even if we felt that on 9/11/01 God was absent, surely we allowed ourselves to feel those things because we needed to have Him in our lives. I hope that we are opening ourselves to allow Him to be in our lives so that others will know that He is present because they see Him in us, and through us.

I hope that we are wise enough to know the difference between God's righteous judgment and hateful revenge and courageous enough to allow for God's righteous judgment. Needless to say, there has been and will continue to be much talk about war and the price that is paid for freedom. There is a place for that. There is a time for that. Now may be the time. I only hope that we are wise enough to know the right time, and open enough to God's leading should we discover we are in the wrong.

I hope that those who are children of God are becoming more aware of and committed to the fact that our identifying mark is love. We are to be identified not by our name, our power, our political party or view, it is not possessions or position, it is not correctness, nor is it the company we keep. Our mark that identifies us as God's children is that we love one another as God has loved us (John 13).

I hope that those who have suffered most and lost the most due to the events of 9/11/01 are being surrounded by those who love them and can guide them to the comforting arms of God. I hope and pray that as God's people we will be instruments in His hands to provide some of that comfort.

I hope that our fears (my fears) will not become so strong that I lose hope in the One who created the world, can calm the storms, and can heal the wounded soul.

> *One thing I ask of the Lord,*
> *this is what I seek:*
> *that I may dwell in the house of the Lord*
> *all the days of my life,*
> *to gaze upon the beauty of the Lord*
> *and to seek him in his temple.*
> *For in the day of trouble*
> *he will keep me safe in his dwelling;*
> *he will hide me in the shelter of his tabernacle*
> *and set me high upon a rock.*
> *Then my head will be exalted*
> *above the enemies who surround me;*
> *at his tabernacle will I sacrifice with shouts of joy;*
> *I will sing and make music to the Lord.*
> (Psalm 27:4-6)

I have some fears, but my hope is in the Lord.

Only A Past

Has this ever happened to you? You run into a friend you have not seen in quite a long time. You recognize one another. You greet one another. You talk about how you both look the same after all these years (even though he's gotten a lot grayer and heavier). You share a few stories of the good old days. You laugh about "what we did back then." Then there is a terribly long and uncomfortable silence. You have nothing else to say. He has gone one way with his life, you have gone another. You say goodbye and "We need to get together," but you realize that will probably never happen. Your only common ground is the past. There is no future. There is only a past.

As sad as the above scenario is, it is not at all uncommon, is it? There are people we have known in the past, but the relationship never grew. In their mind, you are still that skinny kid who sat next to them in English class. In your mind, she is still that girl you hung out with a few times. Beyond that, there is nothing to the relationship.

Even sadder are those relationships that were meaningful. You were really close. You did so much together. You talked about how "No matter what, we'll always keep in touch!" But you didn't. Months passed. Then it was years. Now, you cannot remember the last time you visited. The time, the distance, and the lack of attention have stolen the relationship.

It is tragic when the relationship that has only a past is a member of your family. Your son or daughter. Your mother or father. Your brother or your sister. Your wife or your husband. You look at them and try to talk, but nothing comes. You want to look ahead, but the pain from the past is just too much to overcome. You want to forgive them and make a clean start, but you can't. You know you should, but you cannot find the energy or the desire.

Still more tragic is when the relationship that is described as having no future, only a past, is your relationship with God. Your actions have taken you away from Him. Your lifestyle has left Him in the past. You wonder if there is any way to reconnect after all this time and after all you've done.

What can you do? Is there a way to turn a relationship with only a past into one with a future? There is if you want there to be.

There are a number of characters in Scripture who found themselves with what appeared to be only a past.

David had a wonderful past of serving God, and then saw it crumble because of his impulsive actions. God did not intend for that to be the end. He confessed his sin and restored the relationship. There was bright future.

When Paul came face to face with the Lord on the road to Damascus he may have thought his life was over. He was doomed to live in the memory of what he had done against the Lord. The Lord had other plans.

The son in Luke 15 found himself in a distant country, alone, hungry, and content to forever live as a slave. He could not conceive of a future as his father's son. His father had other plans.

The disciples surely thought on that dark Friday afternoon that their lives were over. All they had left of Jesus was the three years they had spent with Him. They had no future. On Sunday morning, they realized that God had other plans.

It is not necessary for our relationships to be lived in the past. There can be a present. There can be a future. We may not see it or have any notion of what the future could hold, but with God we can have a future. There is more than only a past.

Let God lead you into His future for you.

So Weak and Helpless

"Lord, I feel so weak and helpless!" That is the honest cry of the struggling servant. That is the honest cry of one who tries to serve the Creator of the universe but wonders if he has the strength to continue. That is the heart cry of mothers, fathers, sons, and daughters. That is the heart cry of husbands and wives. That is the pleading of the disciple who wants more than anything to faithfully follow God, but who is growing weary, confused, and wondering if he has what it takes to overcome.

"Lord, I feel so weak and helpless!" says the wife who has become increasingly suspicious that "something is going on" with her husband. "He's not the same man I married. He's saying things and doing things that I never imagined." She is scared. She is confused. She is wondering how much longer this will go on.

"Lord, I feel so weak and helpless!" says the father as he watches his son makes one more decision that will lead him farther from home. He has prayed constantly since before the boy was born that he would be a good father. That he would have wisdom. That he would be able to guide his son as God would have him to. Now he's wondering what he did wrong.

"Lord, I feel so weak and helpless!" says the man who is struggling to keep his business going. He has integrity. He believes in doing what is right, but the "good guy" seems to be coming in last. He is not sure how much longer he can hold on.

"Lord, I feel so weak and helpless!" says the single mom who must be mom, dad, friend, disciplinarian, and spiritual leader for the children she has been left to care for. She's committed to bringing them to church regularly, but even that has become a battleground.

"Lord, I feel so weak and helpless!" says the teenage boy and girl who have made up their mind to keep their relationship pure. They are committed to God, to themselves, and to each other. But the temptation is strong. Plus, practically all their friends have chosen the easier road.

They struggle to do what they know is right.

"Lord, I feel so weak and helpless!" says the church leader after he has received a call from the scared confused wife. "Lord, I feel so weak and helpless!" says the church leader after visiting with the father who is questioning his role as a father. "Lord, I feel so weak and helpless!" says the church leader after talking with the man about his business. "Lord, I feel so weak and helpless!" says the church leader after a brief and tearful visit with the single mom. "Lord, I feel so weak and helpless!" says the church leader after visiting with his own son about the commitment he and his girlfriend have made to have a Godly relationship.

"Lord, I feel so weak and helpless!"

God hears the cries.

He responds, *"My grace is sufficient for you, for my power is made perfect in weakness."*

To keep me from becoming conceited because of these surpassingly great revelations, there was given me a thorn in my flesh, a messenger of Satan, to torment me. Three times I pleaded with the Lord to take it away from me. But he said to me, "My grace is sufficient for you, for my power is made perfect in weakness." Therefore I will boast all the more gladly about my weaknesses, so that Christ's power may rest on me. That is why, for Christ's sake, I delight in weaknesses, in insults, in hardships, in persecutions, in difficulties. For when I am weak, then I am strong. – 2 Corinthians 12:7-10

His grace is sufficient.

I Can't Explain or Fix It

I wish I could claim it as wisdom, but it may simply be a result of the aging process. Whatever the reason, as my journey continues I am finding more and more occasions when I admit, "I can't explain it" and "I can't fix it." It is not a cop-out. I have simply learned that some things I can't explain and some things I can't fix. There was a time when I wanted to do both.

I can't explain how a man who has been married for fifteen or twenty or thirty years and has been a good father can say, "I don't love you any more" and walk away from his family – and be happy. I know it happens. I see it far too often. But I cannot explain how he does it. I'm not sure I really want to know how he does it, but I certainly can't explain it.

I can't explain how Christians who claim to be about His business can get so sidetracked that they spend more time criticizing what others are doing than they spend telling people how much God loves them. The mission shifts from telling the good news about Jesus to telling the bad news about other churches.

I can't explain why some people are healed from their diseases and some are not.

I can't explain why some people seem determined to make the wrong decisions.

I can't explain or comprehend how anyone could ever intentionally harm a child.

I can't explain the power of sin to entice, disrupt, and destroy a life. I know it exists. I know it is real. I am faced daily with the consequences, and I am engaged daily in the battle myself, but I can't explain it.

I can't fix a marriage. When a couple has spent too many years, fought too many wars, missed too many meals, said too many hurtful words, and given too little attention to their relationship, there is no quick and easy fix. I can counsel. I can offer suggestions. I can instruct. I can pray. I can listen. I can offer hope. God can fix it – if given the opportunity. I can't fix a marriage.

I can't fix a life. I want to. I want to fix mine. I want to fix a lot of lives. I want to undo all the mistakes and make right all the wrong decisions. I want to make all the hurt go away and fill the life with love, joy, and peace. But I can't. God can. I can't.

I can't fix a broken heart. I can say, "Time heals all wounds," but does that help? I can comfort. I can console. I can listen. I can offer insights and share Godly wisdom. But I can't fix a broken heart.

I can't explain why I have been so blessed. I have a personal and secure relationship with the Creator of the universe. I have a wonderful family, a lovely home, a fine job, more than enough food, two working automobiles, excellent medical care when I need it, great friends, a place and time to write, and an abundance of good books to read. I can't explain that, but I am grateful for it.

I can't fix the reality that some people do not have those things, or that those who do have them are not aware they have them. I cannot fix it, but I can work toward improving it.

The longer I live the more I am realizing that there are many things I cannot explain and many things I cannot fix. But along with these realizations I am also learning that there is One who can explain and One who can fix. The explanations may not come in this life. The solutions may not be revealed while we inhabit these mortal bodies. But He will explain. He will make all things right. He will do things as He sees fit. I can live with that.

I find comfort in the fact that He has not called me to explain or fix. He has called me to love. He has called me to live my life in such a way that He may use me to help others accept the fact that there are some things no one can explain and only He can fix. I can do that.

Make it your ambition to lead a quiet life, to mind your own business and to work with your hands, just as we told you, so that your daily life may win the respect of outsiders and so that you will not be dependent on anybody. – 1 Thess. 4:11-12

Praise be to the God and Father of our Lord Jesus Christ, the Father of compassion and the God of all comfort, who comforts us in all our troubles, so that we can comfort those in any trouble with the comfort we ourselves have received from God.
– 2 Corinthians 1:3-4

He will provide.

Rejoicing with Those Who Rejoice

Rejoice with those who rejoice; mourn with those who mourn. – Romans 12:15

Paul begins the chapter by urging his audience *to offer your bodies as living sacrifices, holy and pleasing to God.* (Romans 12:1) Then he proceeds to describe in very practical terms what this life of a living sacrifice looks like. He gives instruction on proper understanding and use of gifts, sincere love, dealing with difficult people, and living through difficult times. In the midst of these practical ideas on living a God-centered life, he writes, *Rejoice with those who rejoice; mourn with those who mourn.*

Mourning with those who mourn is not usually a problem. When people you love are hurting, the most natural thing in the world is to hurt for and with them. Rejoicing is not always as easy. It does not always feel natural. It is not always what we want to do.

It is not easy to rejoice when your best friend gets the job you wanted – the job you feel you deserved.

It is not easy to rejoice when your friend gets a date with the boy you are in love with, and you end up home alone on Friday night.

It is not easy to rejoice when your neighbor builds the house of your dreams, and you and your family must stay put.

It is not easy to rejoice when your friend's daughter is always in the limelight, and your daughter is always in the background.

It is not easy to rejoice when the other church in town keeps growing, and yours stays the same or continues to lose members.

It is not easy to rejoice when your friend is pregnant again, and you and your husband continue to hope and wait.

It is not easy to rejoice when friends go off on another exotic vacation, and you stay home to work around the house.

It is not easy to rejoice when someone else's kids are always being bragged about, and yours are in always in trouble.

Although it sounds like the right thing to do, rejoicing with those who rejoice is not always the easy thing to do. Maybe that's why God

220

considered it important enough to be included with Paul's instructions to Christians. Why is it so important?

It is important because when something good happens to us we want to share it. Remember that when the Savior was born the message was good news of great joy. What a pity it would be to have great news – the birth of a child, an engagement ring, or a new job – and no one to share it with. God wants us to be able to share good news.

It is important because we need to share the good things in life. There is plenty of sadness. There is always bad news to share. It was Anne Murray who sang several years ago, "We sure could use a little good news today." We still could. When we love someone and want what is best for them, we rejoice with them.

It is important because it demonstrates that we really do want what is best for other people. When we can overcome whatever amount of envy, jealousy, and regret that we may have in our heart and genuinely rejoice when something good happens to someone else, we are showing them that we do really love them.

Chances are good that as you go about your week you will have an opportunity to rejoice with those who rejoice and mourn with those who mourn. Don't miss the opportunity.

Believe Anyway

In Romans 4:18 Paul writes, *When everything was hopeless, Abraham believed anyway, deciding to live not on the basis of what he saw he couldn't do but on what God said he would do. (The Message)*

Have you been there? Everything is hopeless. You cannot believe that any good will come. Maybe it is time to believe anyway.

Your parents have not been getting along. You have heard their arguments. You have heard talk of divorce. You want to believe that your parents will not split up. *When everything was hopeless, Abraham believed anyway.* Will you?

Your marriage is in trouble. You cannot remember the last time you had a meal that did not include an argument. You want to believe that things will get better. But you can't. *When everything was hopeless, Abraham believed anyway.* Will you?

Your boss just handed you a slip telling you that your position with the company is being eliminated. You have been with them since you got out of college. You thought you would retire in this location. You are looking for another job so your family will not be uprooted. But jobs in your field are scarce. You want to believe, but you can't. *When everything was hopeless, Abraham believed anyway.* Will you?

The doctor's visit did not go well. The news was not what you wanted or expected to hear. What you feared is now coming true. You pray for a miracle. You want to believe something will happen, but all the information says to give up. *When everything was hopeless, Abraham believed anyway.* Will you?

Your church is on the verge of a major blow-up. One group thinks their way is right and only their way is right. Another group thinks their way is right and only their way is right. Tempers flare. Threats are made. Pride is in control. You want to believe that love will conquer and the unity of the body will survive. You want to believe but each discussion makes it more difficult. *When everything was hopeless, Abraham believed anyway.*

Will you?

I don't know what you are facing this week. If your hope is fading and you are wondering if things will ever get better, if you are on the verge of quitting, remember: *When everything was hopeless, Abraham believed anyway.* Will you?

How do we do it? How do we hope anyway when everything thing is hopeless? We again follow Abraham's example. Abraham decided *to live not on the basis of what he saw he couldn't do but on what God said he would do.* Perhaps you should stop looking at what you cannot do and focus instead on what God will do. In Him is hope.

When everything is hopeless, believe anyway.

A Broken Mug

One of my favorite coffee mugs was broken this week. Not sure how it happened. Just found it sitting there on the counter with the handle broken off. A friend had given it to me because it has one of my favorite Bible verses on it. *I press toward the mark for the prize of the high calling of God.* – Philippians 3:14 (*King James Version*)

As I stood there looking with disappointment at my handle-less cup, I realized that now the mug actually illustrates the verse. Before it was a very nice coffee cup with a really meaningful verse on it. Now it may represent what Paul had in mind when he penned the words.

Not that I have already obtained all this, or have already been made perfect, but I press on to take hold of that for which Christ Jesus took hold of me. Brothers, I do not consider myself yet to have taken hold of it. But one thing I do: Forgetting what is behind and straining toward what is ahead, I press on toward the goal to win the prize for which God has called me heavenward in Christ Jesus. – Philippians 3:12-14

Coffee mugs are made with a purpose. Mugs are made for drinking coffee, for drinking hot chocolate, for holding pens, for collecting change. They are not made to simply sit on a shelf and gather dust. When you use a mug, there is the possibility that it will get damaged or broken.

Like the coffee mug, we were created with a purpose. We were created for life. We were not created to sit and watch life go by. We were created to embrace life. Jesus said He came that we *may have life, and have it to the full.* (John 10:10) Paul said we were created to do *good works.* (Ephesians 2:10) The abundant life does not happen without risks. Doing good works is not without dangers.

Life is for living. When you live life, there are risks. When you live, you may get hurt. When you live, you may experience disappointments. When you live, you may get damaged. When you live, you may get broken.

When that happened to Paul, he chose to press on. He did not allow his life to end with a broken handle. He kept pushing forward. He continued to move forward toward the prize God had called him to.

My mug with no handle will most likely be reassigned to be a penholder or a change cup. It has served me well. Many good cups of coffee have been consumed from that mug. But it is time for this mug to move on to a new goal, a new purpose for being.

What about you? Has life been unkind to you lately? Have you considered retiring, sitting out the fight, being shelved? Please don't.

Take a lesson from my mug. Even if your handle gets broken – press on. Move forward. Your handle is broken, but you are not dead. Keep living. God has something in store for you.

Hope Emerges

It has been seven weeks since we had the house fire. In some ways, it seems as if it just happened. In some ways, it seems like a lifetime ago. In some ways, it seems as if it never happened. To say that these have been challenging days would be an understatement. To say that God has blessed us greatly in the midst of the challenge would also be an understatement. In the midst of it all, hope emerges.

I made my routine walk around the house and yard a couple of days ago checking out the latest changes and the progress made since the previous visit. In each visit, I intently look for reasons to be optimistic and signs that this will one day be our home. On this day I found one. Rising from the rubble, ashes and debris, hope still emerges in the form of two brilliant yellow daffodils. The daffodil bulbs were distributed during the memorial service of a young girl last fall. My wife later planted them at the edge of our driveway so that we would see them easily and often. And there they were in the middle of our trampled-down flowerbed filled mostly with weeds, trash, and pieces of broken bricks, two beautiful Lana Beth daffodils. Hope emerges.

That's the way life happens, isn't it? At those times when things seem to be as bad as they can get, hope emerges.

The illness has lasted for weeks. Test results continued to show the progression of the disease. Each day seemed to bring more discouraging news. The medical records had been sent to the best doctors in the world. Nothing changed. Discouragement reigned. Then, out of the blue, a doctor that you had never heard of called saying that he thought he could help. Hope emerges.

The relationship with your parents had become unbearable. Every day brought another explosive battle for independence. They did not understand you. You did not understand them. Nobody seemed to want to understand anybody. You wondered how you would ever survive another week in the house with those people. Then one late and tearful night the conversation made sense. You understood a little about where they were coming from. They understood a little better where you were. Hope emerges.

Things at work could not get worse, or so you thought. Then they did. You dreaded Monday morning. Walking from your car to the office you could feel your stomach churn. When you stepped into the building you expected to feel the same tension that was there when you left on Friday. But something was different. The receptionist smiled differently. The person in the office next to you greeted you kindly, and you returned the greeting. The boss called you and explained that he was aware that things had been bad and that he was willing to work to make them better. Hope emerges.

The marriage that started out with such great potential was in real trouble. You were angry and hurt. She was hurt and angry. You needed help. But there seemed to be none. You both cried yourselves to sleep many nights, and you went through the motions of the day waiting for the next fight. You were both ready to quit. As a last resort, you asked a wise friend for advice. They put their arms around you and prayed. Hope emerges.

Hope emerges all around us. Hope emerged with the birth of Jesus. Hope emerged with the offer of life. Hope emerged with the empty tomb. Hope emerged when we were powerless. Hope emerges with the birth of every child. Hope emerges with every couple that says, "I do." Hope emerges whenever a heart turns to God. Hope emerges with every cup of water that is given to a thirsty soul. Hope emerges whenever a broken heart is lifted. Hope emerges from the darkness. Hope emerges from the ashes. Hope emerges from the rubble. Because He is alive, hope emerges.

The signs of hope are emerging all around you…maybe right in your own front yard.

Goodbye Is Hard

Within a twenty-four-hour period, a young man just out of high school is told that his dad might not survive the disease destroying his body. He was also told that his dog would need to be put to sleep. Goodbye is hard.

The children of their ninety-plus year old mother are told that after all these years, cancer might end her life. Goodbye is hard.

For four years the campus, the local church, and his group of friends have been his home and his family. With graduation comes the move to a new city, the search for a new church, and the quest for new friends. Goodbye is hard.

After nearly a decade of ministry the preacher and his family realize that it's time for a move. The search begins and ends with a move to a new location, a new ministry, and a new community of believers. Goodbye is hard.

For thirty years they have called themselves husband and wife. Suddenly, out-of-the-blue, he informs her that he no longer loves her, he has found someone new, and he wants a divorce. Goodbye is hard.

For more than eighteen years they have cherished every moment of their child's life. They've watched, waited, prayed, and protected her. Today she gets on a plane for a land far away to answer the call of the Lord. Goodbye is hard.

Since before she was born you've been looking forward to and dreading this walk down the aisle. You have practiced your one line, and you have prepared yourself to place her hand into the hand of another man who has promised to provide for her, honor her, protect her, and love her as he loves his own body. You're as ready as you can be. Goodbye is hard.

It's the first day of school and everything is ready. The perfect lunchbox is purchased and packed. The backpack is loaded. You are in the car and headed off to deliver this little one to the first of many strangers who will become major influencers in his life. He walks down the hall, waves goodbye, and disappears into the classroom. You walk away in tears. Goodbye is hard.

The time had come for God to demonstrate the depth of His love for His creation. So, He sent His one and only Son into the world to dwell among His people. He knew what would happen. He knew He would be subjected to ridicule, rejection, suffering, and eventually to carry the burden of the sins of the world. Goodbye is hard.

Someday there will be no more goodbyes. I'm glad. I'm ready.

A Dry Time

A friend of mine calls them dry times. Dry times are those times in your life, more specifically in your spiritual life, when there seems to be a void. A time when all the things you typically do to nourish your soul seem to have stopped working. Some of you understand the dry times very well. You have lived through them. You may be going through one right now. Maybe you have recently come out of such a time. Here are few examples of how a dry time may express itself.

You are going through life pretty much like you always have, but one day things seem different. The sky is not as blue. The breeze is not as cool. The sunshine is not as bright. The snowfall is not as white. Rainbows don't provide much of a thrill. In fact, very few things seem to give your heart much of a thrill.

You are doing the same things you have always done. Except now you are enjoying them less. Very few things seem to excite you. When you try to describe how you feel you use the word "bored" more than you have in a very long time.

Your job once gave you a reason to get up in the morning. It was challenging. It was rewarding. Now it is a job. You go. You put in your time. You come home. Nothing has changed. It is the same job. Nothing has gone wrong. You still like the people you work with, and you still are paid well for your efforts. But it just seems to bore you.

You have a great family. You love them. You would die for them. You long to be with them every opportunity you have. When one visit ends, you begin planning the next one. When you are together you laugh, you cry, you really enjoy your family. You have a wonderful marriage. Your children are healthy. They are doing well in school. Life is good on the home front. But something seems to be missing.

You have an amazing spiritual network. You have been on mission trips with some of them. You have taken vacations with some of them. Your children have grown up together. You have attended weddings, funerals, ball games, parties, seminars, workshops, and baptisms together. You look forward to being with them every opportunity you have. But it seems stale.

Your personal spiritual life seems to be going well. You are doing all the right things. You read your Bible regularly. You pray consistently. You participate in an enriching small group. You occasionally teach a class. You sing on the praise team. You are even thinking about chaperoning a youth trip. You love your church. You love God. You love God's people. But you feel empty.

Songs that once moved you to tears now seem old and tired. Sermons that should touch your heart do not. Prayers seem shallow and repetitious. When people around you are weeping with compassion you are gazing out the window or checking your phone for messages. There is no place you would rather be than in an assembly worshiping God, but you just don't feel anything.

It is a dry time.

What do you do? Where do you go when your well is dry? Where do you go when your heart is empty? Where do you go to find joy? Where do you turn when you need to be refreshed? Where do you go when your soul needs to be restored? Where do you go when you need hope?

John (chapter 4) tells the story about a woman going through a terribly dry time. In fact, dryness was about all she knew. Her home life, if you call it that, was a complete mess. She was lonely. She was rejected. She was isolated. Perhaps the saddest part of her story was that she had reached the point where she was resolved that this was all that her life would ever be. At one time she longed to have a real relationship, but that was so long ago she could barely remember what it was like. As was her routine, when this Samaritan woman needed to refill her water jars she went to the same well where she had always gone for water. She made sure she went during the middle of the day so that she would not bother anyone, and would not be bothered by anyone.

When Jesus initiated a conversation with her she was reluctant. Almost annoyed. Yet, there was something about Him that caught her attention and took her completely by surprise. He seemed to care about her. He had no ulterior motive. He listened to her. He answered her questions. He actually heard her. He knew her even though she had never met Him. He talked to her like a real person. He treated her like she mattered. He gave her hope. He offered her a solution to her dry world. "This water," Jesus said, "if you will drink it will quench your thirst. You'll never be thirsty again. This is living water."

She drank the water.

She came to the well to fill her jars with water. She left having had her dry and empty spirit refilled and refreshed. As she shared her story, others came from their dry world to drink of the living water.

Are you in a dry time? Follow the example of the woman at the well. Spend some time with Jesus. Get alone with Him. Dig into the Word. Go to a place of beauty and soak it in. Be still. Call or visit an old friend. Listen to your favorite music. Take a long walk. Rest. Listen. Play with a child. Serve someone who cannot return the favor.

Drink from the well of living water. After you drink, share your story. You never know who else might be going through a dry time, and God may use you to lead them to the living water.

More Than A Dry Time

What do you do when you do all the things suggested in the previous chapter and nothing changes? You still feel numb, bored, and unmotivated. You still come away from a time of worship, either corporate or private, disappointed and wondering, "What was that all about?"

You read your Bible. You've listened to Christian music everyday while you drive to work. You've not missed an assembly, a small group, or a Bible Class in longer than you can remember. Yet, something is still not right. There may be something deeper, something more than a dry time.

Tom Thompson, writing for the American Association of Christian Counselors, refers to a myth that applies to this situation, "Christians simply need to spend more time in the Word, church, and prayer." The Christian community may be guilty of perpetuating this myth by raising questions "about a person's level of faith or their ability to trust in the Lord." Unfortunately, the message received by the person is often, "If I were only more spiritual, I'd be free from my pain, sickness, or addictions." Thompson goes on to say that there are times when very devoted Christians "need additional tools in order to get unstuck and continue to grow in their spirituality, their relationships, and their personal life. Some have been freed by the 'one-step' process but most of us require additional resources, support and time to work from the inside out."

So, what are you to do when you find you are struggling with something more than a dry time? I offer these suggestions:

Be honest with yourself. It is important to consider that personal sin may be at the root of the issue. Quoting Thompson again: "Again and again, Jesus points out our need to confess and face our sinfulness. Denial is clearly not a biblical option. Scripture tells us, *If we claim to be without sin, we deceive ourselves and the truth is not in us.* (1 John 1:8). And *He who conceals his hatred has lying lips.* (Proverbs 10:18) Religious efforts done by rote

233

without facing our weaknesses become empty rules, lacking *any value in restraining sensual indulgence.* (Colossians 2:23) The good news is that we are safe in the love and grace of God. We can own our badness and not fear condemnation."

Visit your doctor. Physical health may play a part in this issue. When was your last physical exam? Have a check-up. If there is a medical problem, heed the doctor's advice. Take the medicine. Change your diet. Start an exercise program. If the exam shows that you are in good health, the positive news might be enough to boost your spirits and relieve your anxiety.

Talk to someone. Many churches provide counseling services free of charge. Find out if counseling is available. Call for an appointment. With a minimal amount of research, you can find a qualified Christian counselor in your community for a reasonable fee. Fortunately, many insurances companies cover all or part of the fees. If necessary, either of these resources can help you find additional assistance should that be necessary or perhaps direct you to a Christ-centered 12-Step recovery program. The point is, talking helps. Counseling is not a bad thing.

Sometimes we go through dry times. When in a dry time, there are some fairly simple things to do. But sometimes it is more than a dry time. The tried and true methods may fail. You may be experiencing a level of depression or an issue related to your physical health. Remember this: Help is available. You are not alone. God has not deserted you. There are things you can do. Pay attention to the signs and respond in a healthy manner.

Life's Speed Bumps

Although I understand their purpose, I am not a fan of speed bumps. I appreciate their purpose. A speed bump is installed to slow traffic or reduce through traffic. You typically find speed bumps on streets or in shopping center parking lots. They work. Hit a speed bump moving at a high rate of speed and you get bumped. I understand the purpose and appreciate the effectiveness of speed bumps, but I do not like them.

The reason I do not like speed bumps is because they slow me down when I don't want to be slowed down. The street is a shortcut to where I am headed. If I cut through I will make better time. Until they installed speed bumps. The restaurant I am going to is at the far end of the shopping center. I am ready to eat lunch. Because of the speed bumps I must slow down. I am in a hurry. I do not want to slow down. Speed bumps get on my nerves.

Life is filled with speed bumps. Life's speed bumps, like regular speed bumps, appear in places and at times that are inconvenient and particularly unappreciated.

You are moving through life unimpeded and with great ease. Dreams seem to become reality with more consistency than you ever dreamed possible. Then you hit a speed bump. What was to be a routine trip to the doctor to get a prescription filled for what you assumed was a simple seasonal cough, you hit the bump when you heard the doctor say, "I am a little concerned about what I am hearing. I would like to run a few tests to rule out some things."

You have worked hard your entire career to reach a point when you can retire, and you and your wife can travel, visit the grandkids, and go places you have always dreamed about going. You are moving smoothly in that direction when the president of the company invites you to walk with him to his office. "The slumping economy has hurt us all. Our company, though surviving, is having to make some adjustments." You walk slowly back toward your office in shock. The dreams get put on hold.

The church leader knows about speed bumps. Your congregation is thriving. You are seeing real growth – numerical growth and spiritual maturity. Lives are being changed. Souls are being saved. Believers are being encouraged. The future looks bright. Then you hit the bump. A key family decides to go to another church. Another key family learns they are being transferred to another city. You learn that another family has been having serious marital problems for years (unknown to anyone) and have filed for a divorce. One of the most spiritual men in the church, a great teacher and mentor, dies suddenly from a heart attack.

The person who has experienced loss knows about speed bumps. You have had some really difficult days and nights. You wondered if you would ever feel like breathing again. Gradually life returned. You were feeling better. When asked, you would respond, "I'm doing better. I'm doing much better. I think I'm through the worst part." Then bam! It hits. A song, a smell, a movie, a place, or a passing thought jostles your whole being. "Wow! I didn't see that coming."

Your family has gone through some tough times, but you have worked through them with the help of good friends and your church family. You can feel the blessing of healing with each passing day. You thank God every day for what He has done to save your family from destruction. Then in the middle of the night, you get a call from the police.

Speed bumps. You find them in the streets and the parking lots, and you find them in your life. How do you handle them?

Like bumps in the road, you have choices. You can look for another route. Usually there is no other route. You can speed over them hoping that will soften the blow. It does not. So, what do you do with life's speed bumps?

Consider how Paul approached his speed bump:

To keep me from becoming conceited because of these surpassingly great revelations, there was given me a thorn in my flesh, a messenger of Satan, to torment me. Three times I pleaded with the Lord to take it away from me. But he said to me, "My grace is sufficient for you, for my power is made perfect in weakness." Therefore, I will boast all the more gladly about my weaknesses, so that Christ's power may rest on me. That is why, for Christ's sake, I delight in weaknesses, in insults, in hardships, in persecutions, in difficulties. For when I am weak, then I am strong. – 2 Corinthians 12:7-10

Recognize what is happening. Remember that the bump in your path is more likely the work of Satan and not the Father. Paul's thorn was given to "torment" him. The same is true for that speed bump. Satan has put it there because he knows it irritates you, frightens you, discourages you, frustrates you, and has the potential of keeping you from your goal. Do not assume the worst about God. He is not out to get you. He wants to help you. He is on your side. The speed bump can help you slow down and check your options, adjust your direction, and realign your focus.

Rely on God's power. Paul admits that he would have preferred to go a different route. He asked for a different plan. When he realized there was no option, he accepted and drew on God's power when he was weak to sustain him. He even came to *delight in weaknesses, in insults, in hardships, in persecutions, and in difficulties.* When you hit one of life's speed bumps rely on God's power to carry you over it.

As you travel through your day, pay attention. When you come to a speed bump, do not be surprised. Take it slow and move on. When you are weak, then you are strong.

At Just the Right Time

Year-end reflections invariably reveal the remarkable impact of God's providential care of His children. The evidence is impossible to ignore for the conscientious follower of Jesus. If you have not taken inventory of how God has worked in your life over the last twelve months, please reward yourself by acknowledging how God has stepped into your world at just the right time and in just the right way.

Remember how your world seemed to have no meaning when the relationship to end all relationships ended? You were devastated. You were heart broken. You wept. You grieved. You wondered if you would ever laugh again. Then at just the right time a new special person came along, filled the void, and opened new avenues of love and joy that you had never imagined.

Remember that horrible day when your boss told you that he had to terminate your employment? You were stunned. You did not have a clue this was going to happen. Having to go home and tell your wife that you had lost your job was the worst day of your life. Then at the just the right time when you were not sure how you were going to pay your mortgage and health insurance, you got a call from a company offering you a new job, with a higher salary, and better working conditions.

Remember that afternoon when your daughter received the rejection from the university she had dreamed of attending? She dropped the letter, burst into tears, went into her room, and did not come out for hours. She was embarrassed. She was angry. She was sad. She was confused. There was nothing you could do to make things better. You prayed for her. You listened to her when she wanted to talk. Then one day when she was at her lowest, at just the right time, she received an acceptance letter and an offer for a full scholarship at another university. She started in the fall, has a wonderful roommate, and cannot imagine being at the other school.

Remember that Sunday at church when the minister announced he had accepted a ministry position with another church in another state?

The whole church was shocked. He had been here for years. He's the only minister your family has ever known. You wondered if the church would survive. Then at just the right time when you were discouraged and many of the members were grumbling and complaining about how things were, the new man showed up. You loved him immediately. His fresh vision and loving ways has brought new life and vitality to the church.

Remember that morning when your doctor told you he had seen something unusual on some of your scans? You were terrified. You immediately started imagining the worst possible scenarios. They did more tests. Then they did more tests. What they thought they were looking for turned out to be nothing, but while doing the tests they discovered a tumor. Surgery to remove the tumor was completely successful. At just the right time, when you didn't know anything was wrong, your life was saved.

Remember when you committed that horrible sin? The worst sin anyone ever committed. A sin you could not have ever imagined you could commit. You felt awful. In your mind, you could not conceive of anyone being able to forgive you or love you ever again. Then at just the right time when you were absolutely powerless you read these words: *You see, at just the right time, when we were still powerless, Christ died for the ungodly. Very rarely will anyone die for a righteous person, though for a good person someone might possibly dare to die. But God demonstrates his own love for us in this: While we were still sinners, Christ died for us.* – Romans 5:6-8

When we take the time at the end of a year, or any other time, we are likely to discover that God has been working for our good in ways we never dreamed of. And at just the right time, He steps in to do what only He can do to change the course of our lives. Acknowledge His involvement in your life. Give Him credit. Praise His activity in your life. Live the rest of your life as an expression of gratitude for what He did at just the right time.

He Is Risen!

My most vivid childhood memory of Easter involves polishing my shoes. Yes, you read that correctly. Polishing shoes was our Easter ritual that I now realize was a clever way to implement tradition. To me, there was no rhyme or reason to it, but it did serve as an effective way for our parents to get us to shine our shoes on Easter morning.

The understanding in our house was that if you wanted Easter candy on Easter morning, your shoes had to be cleaned, polished, shined, and placed outside your bedroom door. With shoes cleaned and shined, we would go to bed, then on Easter morning we would find our shined shoes miraculously filled with Easter candy, along with a basket full of eggs and more candy. I eventually discovered that the Easter Bunny was just as much of a night owl as Santa was. But none of this mattered, as long as I had an adequate supply of those white, cream-covered eggs with pink, yellow, blue, and green sugar. Such a healthy snack to start off our Sunday morning!

The second most vivid memory of my childhood Easters was dyeing the Easter eggs. Usually on the Saturday before, the eggs would be boiled and tablets of dye would be dropped into heated vinegar. Next, the boiled eggs would be placed on a copper wire with a circle designed specifically to hold one egg at a time. The egg would be dipped into the dye and an amazing transformation would take place. Those plain white eggs became various shades of red, blue, green, yellow, and pink. Some of them came out of the dye with unique designs that we would create with a wax crayon. After the color transformation, the eggs, still wet with warm vinegar, would be placed on newspaper spread out on the kitchen table to dry. I can still here my mom's warnings: "Don't touch them! You'll mess them up! You have to let them dry!"

And so, adequately jacked up on sugar, off we would go to church – dressed in our best (and only) pair of black pants, white shirts, black ties, and beautifully polished shoes – soon to join all the ladies and little girls dressed in their Sunday best, wearing their pretty hats and new fancy dresses.

I suppose the preacher spoke about the Resurrection, but I most likely missed it, falling asleep right about the time he started. But I assure you I woke up in time for the Easter egg hunt that followed. That I would not miss.

Eventually, I outgrew those traditions. Well, most of them. I still try to make sure my shoes are in pretty good shape, and I now prefer the Reece's Peanut Butter bunnies instead of the colorful sugar-coated eggs. I also eventually came to understand that the miracle of Easter was not about candy mysteriously showing up in my shoes or eggs changing color right before my eyes. Easter was about a Savior who had died and been buried and then rose again from His grave.

The miracle is about the followers of Jesus who watched Him suffer pain and humiliation, who witnessed the afflictions of His wounds and declaration of His death, who saw Him conquer death and rise again. Hope restored.

I now understand that an Easter sunrise means more than hunting eggs and wearing my best clothes. It means that the time of darkness has passed and the Light has returned. It means that the hope that had been lost has now returned. It means that although we go through times of waiting and confusion, even despair, because of that empty tomb, hope is restored.

He is risen! He is risen indeed!

The Wondrous Stories We Live

As I waited for the light to change I saw the man selling papers. I see him in the same location on a regular basis. He always smiles a friendly smile. He always waves a friendly wave. He walks along the line of cars, then turns around and comes back to his original station. What was his life like before he came to sell papers on the street? Where is his family? Do they know he is on the street? Do they care? I wonder about his story.

She comes into the sanctuary just as we are beginning each week. She sits in the very back, near an exit. She seems to know most of the songs we sing and appears to enjoy the time in the assembly. But as we are singing the invitation song she quietly slips out unnoticed. I wonder about her story.

If I were to describe him I would use words like rugged, strong, hard, and calloused. None of those would refer to his physical appearance, but his demeanor. My impression is that if I were to ask him about his life, he would say something like, "Oh, I've been around." That would be it. His answer would be saying, "I doubt you really want to know my story." But I do. I wonder about his story.

He comes to church with his parents. He sits with them and stays pretty close to them before and after. Occasionally one of the other children will approach him and invite him to play with them. He always declines and stays close to his mother. He does not really appear to be afraid, but he is not confident enough to venture away. I later learn that he is adopted. I was already wondering about his story, now I wonder about it even more.

Her parents' marriage crumbled when she was very young. Most of her life has been spent going from one parent to the other. Two sets of grandparents. Two different homes. Juggling the holidays and summer vacations. Always trying to be the good girl who never caused trouble. Now, in her late teens, she tries to find her way through the world and tries to discover who she is. When we have talked, she has a look in her eyes that says she wonders where this life she has lived is going to lead, and she wonders who she will be when her story comes to an end. I, too, wonder about her story and where her life will take her.

She is just a child. She is sweet. She is innocent. She is loved and nurtured and protected and nourished by the best parents anyone one could ever ask for. She has a vivid imagination and an abundance of energy. I watch her and I marvel at the story God is weaving with her, for her, and through her.

He was in his early twenties when I met him. He was troubled. He was angry. He acted tough and wanted everyone to think he was tough. Getting beyond the walls of his heart required something I did not have. We spent some time together, and I did what I could; then he disappeared. I often wonder where he is, how he is, and if he is. I wonder if he has ever been able to make sense of his story.

As I wonder about these people, I am in awe that God has allowed me to have a glimpse into their lives. For some, I have played a minor role in their story. For others, I have had a greater influence, just as they have influenced me. They have all touched me, challenged me, blessed me, and opened the eyes of my heart to remind me there is more — much more — to this life than I can see. They have all reminded me that there is more — much more — to this life than me.

We all have a story. Although we may sometimes wonder about where our story is leading, how it is being written, or why it has not taken on a different theme, we do not need to wonder about one thing: He has always been involved, graciously shaping us into the image of His Son.

For those God foreknew he also predestined to be conformed to the image of his Son, that he might be the firstborn among many brothers and sisters. – Romans 8:29

I am Willing

While Jesus was in one of the towns, a man came along who was covered with leprosy. When he saw Jesus, he fell with his face to the ground and begged him, "Lord, if you are willing, you can make me clean." Jesus reached out his hand and touched the man. "I am willing," he said. "Be clean!" And immediately the leprosy left him. – Luke 5:12-13

Have you ever made a request of the Lord similar to that of the man with leprosy? Maybe it did not involve being made clean, but instead you asked for relief from a different kind of suffering. "Lord, if you are willing...

You can heal my addiction.

You can find me a job.

You can help me forgive my brother.

You can help me forgive myself.

You can heal my marriage.

You can help me stop worrying.

You can bring my child home.

You can help me feel loved."

The man's request is a desperate request. It is the request of a man who had wanted to be clean as long as he can remember, maybe longer than he can remember.

You can understand that kind of desperation, can't you? You have been there. You are there. You want to see God work in your life. You long to see God's power in the life of your spouse, in the life of your son or your daughter. So, with a desperate inkling of hope you make your request: "Lord, if You are willing You can..."

With the words barely out of your mouth you hear His response. "I am willing."

"What did You say? You are willing? Are You really?"

He repeats His answer, "I am willing."

It happens. It is done. Perhaps the cure does not come as quickly as with the man with leprosy, but it comes. Your marriage begins to improve. Your relationship with your children improves. Your prodigal calls and wants to come home. You begin to realize you are loved by God and by God's people. Your unforgiving spirit begins to soften. You begin to understand that God is more merciful toward you than you dreamed possible, and maybe you can be forgiven and restored.

As you think about it, you know it is God because these things could not happen any other way. There was no other hope than your hope in God. Everything else had been tried and failed. God did it.

That is the kind of God He is. He is a God who says, "I am willing."

Will you listen to Him say, "I am willing?" He wants to help. He wants to heal. He wants to restore. He is willing. Will you let Him help?

Part Four
Reflecting

By experiencing the love of Jesus, the dream of being one of His followers emerges. By following Jesus, we discover the power and beauty of His reign on earth as it is in Heaven. By reflecting on Jesus, we realize that all our hopes and dreams are fulfilled through our relationship with Him.

For now we see only a reflection as in a mirror; then we shall see face to face. Now I know in part; then I shall know fully, even as I am fully known.
1 Corinthians 13:12

My prayer is that as you reflect on what God has done in your life that you will find peace and discover the vision of what He wants to do in, around, and through you.

Thank You for Being Kind to Me

At the end of an interview with a fairly well-known preacher about significant events of the twentieth century, the man being interviewed said, "Thank you for being kind to me." Due to a particular incident in his ministry, I suspect he has experienced his share of unkindness. So, his gratitude for someone being kind to him was no doubt genuine.

I turned off the tape, but I continued thinking about the man's words as I drove down the street. "Thank you for being kind to me." Those words stayed with me, reminding me of people who need to hear those words from me.

To the person in the parking lot who might have wanted the parking spot I got, thank you for being kind to me.

To the cashier in the grocery store who was courteous to me even when I was not so courteous to her, thank you for being kind to me.

To the doctors who have examined me, treated me, operated on me, medicated me, and reassured me, thank you for being kind to me.

To the nurse in the intensive care unit after my surgery who treated me with such care that I wondered if she might be an angel, thank you for being kind to me.

To the other nurse who worked with me and helped me learn to suck through a straw when I was very, very frustrated, thank you for being kind to me.

To the parents who gave me life (even though they are no longer here and able to read these words), taught me the meaning of family, showed me the way to live, and started me on this journey, thank you for being kind to me.

To the friends who knew me when I was not nearly as mature as I am today (and those who know I am not nearly as mature as I think I am today), who accepted me when I felt unacceptable, who loved me when I felt absolutely unlovable, and believed in me when I felt there was very little to believe in, thank you for being kind to me.

To the teachers and mentors who saw something in me that I could not see, encouraged me to try when I did not want to try, taught me even when they did not realize they were teaching, complimented me even when there was not much to compliment, and helped me reach the point where I could teach others, thank you for being kind to me.

To the brothers and sister who have known me since the beginning, tolerated me as a child, accepted me as an adult, and still seem to enjoy being with me, thank you for being kind to me.

To the two children who have obeyed me, listened to me, talked to me, played with me, wanted to be with me, accepted me when I was tired and discouraged, loved me, helped me know the joys of being a dad, and helped me learn so much about how our Heavenly Father must think of us, thank you for being kind to me.

To the woman who married me almost twenty-four years ago, has walked with me, beside me, encouraged the good she saw in me, endured the bad she saw in me, loved me, shared life with me, and been patient with me, thank you for being kind to me.

To the people who have listened to me preach for the last thirteen years and complained very little, thank you for being kind to me.

To the people who have read *A Norvell Note*, shared it with others, and still read, thank you for being kind to me.

To the God who knew me before I was born, knows the words I will speak or write before they are formulated in my mind, understands me even when I don't understand myself, protects me, guides me, has saved me, is preparing a place for me, and demonstrates in more ways than I can ever imagine how much He loves me, thank you for being kind to me.

Enjoy the kindness.

The Last Time

My family is in the middle of a move, so we are finding ourselves doing things and going places and saying, "This will be the last time we will ever do this."

We went to beach for the last time. I preached for the last time. I wrote my last bulletin article. We visited our neighbors for the last time. We ate with friends for the last time.

We hope to do several things one more time. We would like to make it to our favorite Mexican restaurant one last time. We would like to visit our favorite park one last time. We want to take a walk through our neighborhood one last time. If we have a chance, we will probably stop by our favorite ice cream shop for a milk shake. Add to all the things already mentioned, there are all the people we are seeing for what may be the last time. I would like to play a round of golf with my friends one last time.

When we do something for what may be the last time we tend to view it differently. We want to make a mental photograph that will never fade. We want to listen to every word. We want to hold on to every image and every comment and every relationship. Events that never really seemed significant suddenly take on a whole new meaning. We fear that food will never taste so good, skies will never be so blue, winds will never be as fresh, or love will never be as real.

I wonder if Jesus felt any of those things as He approached the cross. Do you suppose when He walked through the streets a few days before His death He spoke to people and thought, "I will never do this again." Or, do you suppose when He visited the synagogue He thought about how he might be doing it for the last time? I like to imagine that He did think those things and feel those things.

But one thing I do know. When Jesus finished His walk through the streets, reached the place of the skull, breathed His last breath on the cross, and came out of the grave three days later, His message for us was this is the last time anyone will ever need to be afraid of death. This is the last time you will need to mourn at the death of a believer. This is the last time you will have to wonder what will happen to you. From now on you can rest in peace because of the sacrifice that was given for the last time.

Doing things for the last time is an emotionally draining and physically tiring experience. But unless we do some things for the last time, we cannot do other things for the first time. Because we have been afraid of death for the last time means we can approach life with joy and hope and excitement maybe for the first time. Because we have said goodbye to sin for the last time means we can say hello to newness of life for the first time.

As we go through the process of moving to a new location we are doing many things for the last time, and the tears will flow. But in a few days we will begin doing many other things for the first time, and more tears will flow.

Enjoy the day, even if it is for the last time.

Better Left Unheard

Through the years I have probably filled several journal pages being thankful for the ability to hear. I am learning also to be thankful for some of the things I do not hear. Here are some examples of things I am thankful I do not hear.

I am thankful I do not hear all the negative things said, thought, and felt about my writing, preaching, and teaching. Even a single comment can send me into a tailspin of questioning and self-doubt.

I am thankful I do not hear all the things the "other drivers" have to say about my driving. Reading lips is quite sufficient.

I am thankful I do not hear all the things my children say about me, especially after they have been disciplined. The look in their eyes says plenty.

I am thankful I do not hear more vulgarities and foul language. Standing in line for a cup of coffee can provide me with language I never cared to hear.

I am thankful I do not hear all the times people make fun of me. I have heard enough to understand the pain it can cause and remind me to be thoughtful of others.

I am thankful I do not hear any more compliments than I hear. One or two can inflate my ego to a dangerous level.

I am thankful I do not hear all the cries for help that my Father hears. He knows how much I can handle and thankfully limits the number that I hear.

I am thankful I do not hear any more noise than what I do hear. I hear enough to make me appreciate a quiet morning.

I am thankful I do not hear more long periods of silence from the Lord than I do. Short periods of silence are enough to frighten me and cause me to question my relationship with Him.

I am thankful I do not hear the Lord condemn me, reject me, or tell me He no longer loves me. He knows I could not handle those words.

Jesus said, *"Whoever has ears, let them hear."* (Matthew 11:15) He wants us to listen. But He also knows we cannot bear to hear all the sounds that He hears. He knows that for us, some things are better left unheard. He hears it all.

Thankful I don't hear what I don't need to hear.

More Forgiving and A Bigger Sweet Spot

It has been my custom since beginning *A Norvell Note* to start each year with an article that has something to do with golf. I am not exactly sure why I did that, but that is how this all started on January 5, 1998. So, not wanting to break with tradition, here is a lesson I have learned from a new golf club.

Last fall, through the kind generosity of a dear friend (Thanks Dan) I was invited to play in a golf tournament at one of the most exclusive country clubs in our area. When you play in charity tournaments you usually receive a goodie bag filled with prizes donated by merchants in the area. In the tournaments I typically play, the contents of the goodie bag consists of a couple of bags of crackers, a coupon for a free golf lesson, and maybe a towel or sleeve of golf balls. This tournament was different, and this goodie bag was really different. Among the very nice free items I received, I was given the choice between a very expensive putter and a very expensive driver. Having watched one of my playing partners that day putt with this style putter for eighteen holes I decided to go with the driver. A King Cobra SS 427. The head cover alone is probably worth more than my old set of woods.

Like a child with a new toy I headed off to share my good fortune with everyone I saw. I could not wait to try it out. As time passed, I did try it out, and it has helped my game. But that is not the lesson I want to share with you. A couple of months after receiving the new driver I saw a full-page ad in a national newspaper about my new club. Among the numerous selling points, the advertisement described how this new club "tested incredibly long and forgiving," something a golfer like me is always interested in (and in need of). Then at the bottom of the page the ad read, "We're not talking about a sweet spot, we're talking about a sweet zip code." That is what caught my eye.

If a golf club manufacturer can develop a driver with a larger sweet spot and is more forgiving, I wondered if I should consider doing the same. I wondered, what if, as the new year begins I began to demonstrate that I, a child of God, am new and improved? What if I show that I have a bigger sweet spot and I am more forgiving? What if I used this golf club as a reminder of not only a way to improve my golf game but also a way to improve my life?

With a more forgiving attitude I will not hold grudges. I will let go of offenses against me. I will ignore more comments. I will not assume the worst in people. I will not hang on to their mistakes. I will not remind them of the mistakes they have made, the flaws I see, and wrongs they have done. I will be more forgiving of myself. I will allow God to truly free me of my sins. I will let go of my past and enjoy the experience of being new.

With a bigger sweet spot in my heart I will be open to more of the blessings God sends my way. I will notice the small things He places in my path. I will spend more time with children. I will listen more, try to understand more, and affirm others more often. I will guide more and inform less. I will suggest more and dictate less. I will touch people with more gentleness, hold on to them more loosely, and release them with more confidence, hope, and love. With a bigger sweet spot, I will sing more, smile more, hug more, encourage more, and enjoy more.

As you can see, not only do I hope to see better numbers on my score card in the coming year, but I also hope you see a better me, a more forgiving me, a nicer me. I hope you see me with a bigger sweet spot. I also hope that if you need to make similar changes that you will not wait to receive a new golf club. Just start making the changes.

Start the New Year with a bigger sweet spot.

Life at Fifty

I wanted my fiftieth birthday to be something special. I wanted it to be something more than just another day, than just another birthday. Fifty years old. Wow! Fifty is one of those milestones of life that is almost always out front in the far distant future. Not anymore. As I approached the half-century mark, I wanted to find something that might help commemorate this time in my life. I searched for words or phrases that could possibly help summarize my fifty years or help characterize my first fifty years.

I thought perhaps the words of some of our great leaders might hold the key. I came across this quote by Thomas Jefferson, "The sun has not caught me in bed in fifty years." As I crawl out of bed on most mornings well after the sun has risen, I realize that certainly does not characterize my life. I sought the wisdom of those who have passed this milestone about how I am supposed to feel at this point in life and received this response: "Old!" With that wealth of information, I decided to simply reflect on what I have experienced and offer a few observations on life at fifty.

I am not in control. There are many things that are beyond my control. As each year passes, I realize there are more things beyond my control. How people plan for me to celebrate my fiftieth birthday is beyond my control. The weather is beyond my control. War is beyond my control. Whether a friend chooses to live or die is beyond my control. Whether disease attacks my body or the body of someone I love is beyond my control. About all I can control is how I respond to the things that happen.

I have only one opportunity to do some things. Some of the most important things happen only once. I held my son and my daughter for the first time only once. I saw my bride walking down the aisle only once. I turned sixteen only once. I drove a car for the first time only once. There is only one first day of the week. I should have tried to snow ski only once.

I baptized my children only once. Special moments with children happen only once. Conversations with friends happen only once. I will turn fifty only once. So many of the truly significant events in life come quickly and pass quickly. I do not want to miss the opportunity to enjoy them to the fullest.

I do not control the clock. Most things do not happen on my time schedule. I may make plans, I may keep my calendar full and my life on schedule, but I must realize that it is my schedule. The Lord controls the clock. I may try to slow things down, and I may try to speed things up, but it does no good. I may even rush through life, but I cannot rush life. It happens at God's speed, on God's terms, and on His schedule. Healing takes place on God's schedule. Prayers are answered on God's schedule. Changes of the heart come on His schedule. Dreams come true on His schedule. Broken hearts are mended on His schedule.

Because many things are beyond my control, and because some of the most important things happen only once, and because most things are on God's schedule, I have arrived at this conclusion: I want to make the most of every moment of my life. I really don't want to waste another minute. I found these words in Psalm 90:12: *Teach us to number our days, that we may gain a heart of wisdom.*

Father, I'm fifty years old. Use me today and the rest of my life for Your glory.

With Another Step

With his first step, we knew life would never be the same. We knew from that point on he would be exploring the world, growing more independent, testing the limits, and becoming his own person. As he took that first step, his mother and I prayed: "God lead him, protect him, and help him to get back up when he falls." That was a long time ago.

With another step, he walked into the world of education. We were cautious about leaving him too soon as it was a new city for us all. He had never met the teacher, he had never been to the school, and he did not know another child in the class. But when we opened the door and the teacher greeted him, he stepped in, waved goodbye and walked off into the class.

With another step, he walked into the world of sports. With one step, he learned to play basketball. With one step, he crossed home plate. With another step, he headed down the soccer field. With another step, he tackled the quarterback. Step by step, he played, we watched. One step at a time he learned to play and eventually learned to give a play by play.

With another step, he walked into the world of spiritual things. He heard the message. His heart was touched. He was convicted that a decision must be made. He walked into the water and was raised to new life.

With another step, he walked into the world of relationships. Friendships. Romantic relationships. Spiritual relationships. Work relationships. Some were good relationships and have lasted through the years. Others were not so good and lasted only a short time. He learned to love, to encourage, to give, and to receive.

With another step, he walked into the world of responsibility. He learned to work hard. He learned to deal with frustrations on the job. He learned to be a person of his word. He learned honesty and integrity.

With another step, he walked into the world of tragedy. He had known hurt and disappointment. He had known what it meant to lose. But he had never known this kind of hurt, and he had never known this kind of loss. As he took this step, he learned to deal with anger, bitterness, and grief.

With another step, he walked into the world of the university. He found his direction and listened to his heart. He eventually found his passion and began to pursue it. He studied hard but not too hard. He enjoyed his time. He made new friends and maintained old friends. He searched his heart and stretched his mind. He broadened his horizons and developed his dream.

Now, with another step he has crossed the stage and received his degree. He is headed out into the world to work, to make a difference, to start his own family. As he took those steps across the stage, his mother and I prayed, as we have done with every step he has taken: "Dear God, lead him, protect him, and help him to get back up when he falls."

Dear God, lead us, protect us, and help us get back up when we fall.

No Place to Sleep

A few weeks ago, I spent an extended period of time pondering all the things I had convinced myself that I needed that I did not already have. During my private "I wish…" and "If only…" party I developed quite a list of things that I was convinced were essential if my life were to be complete. You may know the routine. You may have a similar list.

My thinking went something like this: "Everyone else has a new car, why am I driving a ten-year old model?" "Man, a pool sure would be nice." "Those folks down the street just built a huge new church building, and man, what a nice parking lot." "I wonder what it would be like to be a member of that country club?" "How do those people afford to take such extravagant vacations?" "That new computer will do everything I will ever want to do!" Have you been down that road? Have you ever spent any time on the "I-wonder-what-would-be-like-highway?"

I was cruising along minding my own business when all of a sudden my daydreaming came to an end. It was late in the day. I was the only person at the building when Anthony came in. He sat for a while. I listened to his story. He had just moved to our area and was looking for work. He was trying to get back on his feet and make a new start in a new location. He had spent a few nights in a local motel, but his money had run out before his need for a place had been met. He was desperate. I pulled out my wallet, gave him a little cash, and told him if he did not find something to come back the next day. He left. I did not see him the next day. I sat there in my office thinking: "I'm focused on cars, buildings, computers, and me…Anthony doesn't have a place to stay."

I don't need a lecture on how unwise it is to give cash to strangers. I know that he "may have gone to the first liquor store he came to." I don't need to be reminded of all the "other agencies" out there who can really help people like that. I don't even need anyone to tell me how blessed I am to be able to reach in my wallet and find cash to share with a stranger. I know all that.

What I need is a way to get my eyes off myself, my stuff, my things, my wants, my needs, and think about others on a more consistent basis. What I need is to find a way to stop (at least slow) my desire for more things. What I need is some way to be less consumed by the things of this life and more concerned about the people who need life. What I need is some way to stop thinking about all the stuff I want while Anthony has no place to sleep.

I have some needs. God is generously providing for those needs. I have lots of wants. More than anything I want to be like Jesus. But I also want to help Anthony find a place to sleep.

Lord, help me!

A Prayer from Parents

Letting Go

Dear Father of all nations and Creator of all things, we come to You on behalf of our child. You gave us this child almost two decades ago with the understanding that we would care for him until he was ready to leave our home and go off into the world on his own. He says he is ready. In a few days, he will be graduating from high school. He says he is ready for his independence. He says he is ready and able to take care of himself. He says he ready; we are not so sure.

Father, we have tried to do things according to Your plan. We have loved her. We have taken her to church and even gone with her. We have taught her Your truths in our home. We have taken every precaution we were aware of in order to ensure that Your word would be imbedded into her heart and soul. We have done all that, yet we are still frightened at the idea of her being on her own. We are eager for her to make her own way, but we wonder if we have missed something. We wake up early and lie awake well into the night reliving conversation after conversation hoping we have not forgotten anything. She says she is ready to go; we are not so sure.

Father, as we watch him prepare for these never-again-to-be-repeated activities we struggle with what is ahead. We know we are to "Seek first your Kingdom," and we have tried and continue to do that. With all our might we have tried to love You and serve You. We have tried, yet we know we have failed many times along the way to live like You would have wanted us to live. We are grateful for the way Your grace has covered us, and Your presence has carried us during those times when we were completely helpless and totally clueless. Father, he says he is ready, but we are not so sure.

Father, we are not doing a very good job in this area of letting go. We thought we were prepared for it. Of course, during those times when she exerts her independent spirit, we think we may actually be ready for her to be out of the house. Then we think about how it will be when she is gone; her room will be empty, the music will not be too loud, the washing machine will get a rest, and the phone may be for one of us, if it rings at all. She says she is ready, but we are not so sure.

Father, in a few days we will hear his name called, and he will walk across the stage, receive his diploma, celebrate with his friends, and begin to finalize plans to leave in the fall. We will not know where he is all the time. We will not know the friends he will spend time with. His car will not be parked in the driveway. We will go out to eat without him, and we will come home without him. Father, he says he is ready, but we are not so sure.

Father, we have prayed for her every day since we realized we were going to have a baby. We have watched her grow, and we have done everything we knew to do to prepare her for what lies ahead. Now, we pray that we have done our job well. We will never know unless we let her go. She says she is ready, but we are not so sure.

Father, we place our children in Your hands. Of that one thing, we are sure.

Cap and Gown

It seems like only a few months ago that I held her in my arms for the first time. She wore the little cap that babies wear in the hospital nursery. Not long after that she was wearing gowns to sleep in and to twirl around in like a ballerina. Now, she's wearing a cap and gown of a different color and style as she walks across the stage to receive her high school diploma. Has this really happened? How can it be that this little one who once curled up in my lap as I rocked her to sleep is now marching in with her classmates to the tune of the familiar graduation ceremony music?

Between the time when she wore a cap and gown as a little girl and now as a beautiful young woman, we have shared many times of joy and times of sadness. We have laughed together; we have cried together. We have shared secrets. We have taken walks and have ridden our bikes through neighborhoods and along the beach. She has learned to ride horses, play sports, drive a car, cheer for the home team, have her first date and many others since then. She has grown from a little girl who said she would never move away from home to a young lady who is eager to be in a dorm room and expand her level of independence.

Like moms and dads all over the country, as we watch her today her mother and I fight back the tears as we realize our hold on her is becoming less and less each day. It started with sleepovers, then she began taking trips with her friends without us, then there were shared meals with the family and friends, trips to the local breakfast place before school, banquets, chorus concerts, and ball games. Soon it will be foreign mission trips, college orientation, packing her things, and decorating her dorm room.

There's a part of me that wants to cry out, "Stop! This cannot be happening! It's too soon. She's not ready. I'm not ready!" There's another part of me that loves to look at the beautiful young lady, thank God for whom she has become, and long to see what God has in store for her over the next phase of her life. There's still another part of me that just wants to take her in my arms again and comfort her when she's afraid, dry her tears when she cries, and reassure her that she will always be loved. There's yet another part of me that wishes I could freeze this moment in time and forever enjoy it, or, better yet, rewind the last eighteen years.

But as John Ortberg reminds us in *When the Game Is Over, It All Goes Back in the Box*, "Life does not have a rewind button." (Ortberg, John. *When the Game Is Over, It All Goes Back in the Box*. Zondervan, 2015.) I cannot turn back the clock. She must grow. She must go. She must learn. She must earn her own way. She must experience life for herself and learn some of the hard lessons of life all on her own. There will be times she will cry, and I will not be there to dry her tears. There will be days when she seeks the advice of another. There will be times when I will wonder if she has forgotten what we had? Will she remember how special our relationship is? There will be times when I'll miss her so much that my heart and my soul will ache. Maybe there will be times when she misses me, too.

I accept the reality that today she wears a cap and gown, walks across the stage on graduation day, and is on her way to being a woman. Yet, in my mind and in my heart, she will always be the sweetest little girl in the whole wide world, and I pray that she remembers these words I sang to her:

> She's the sweetest girl in the whole wide world.
> There's not a doubt in my mind.
> When I look at her and see her smile,
> I'm so proud she's mine.
> She's the sweetest girl in the whole wide world,
> There's not a doubt in my mind.
> When she looks at me and she makes me smile,
> I thank the Lord she's mine.

Friends

Jesus said, *"My command is this: Love each other as I have loved you. Greater love has no one than this, that he lay down his life for his friends. You are my friends if you do what I command. I no longer call you servants, because a servant does not know his master's business. Instead, I have called you friends, for everything that I learned from my Father I have made known to you. You did not choose me, but I chose you and appointed you to go and bear fruit—fruit that will last. Then the Father will give you whatever you ask in my name. This is my command: Love each other."* (John 15:12-17)

Father, You have blessed me in more ways than I could have ever asked or imagined. You have given me good health, and when I have had poor health You have provided excellent health care for me that enables me to heal. You have provided me with enough wealth to supply my needs; and when I have wanted more than my needs, You have blessed me with many luxuries. You have blessed me with a wonderful family, and when I think I could not be more blessed, You increase my family and add more blessings. Thank You.

As I reflect on my blessings and think my heart could be no fuller, You share more of Your goodness and love by giving me friends.

You have given me friendships that have endured decades and weathered storms.

You have given me friendships that have survived selfishness and neglect from both sides.

You have given me friendships that weathered storms and experienced seasons of overflowing joy.

You have given me friends who have stood by me in times of struggle, stood with me in times of battle, who have stood in front of me in times of attack, and who have held me up when I grew weary and wanted to quit.

You have given me friends who have spoken words of love and backed those words up with action.

You have given me friends who have avoided the talk about love but who have instead simply loved.

You have given me friends who have laughed with me, wept with me, hurt with me, sat in confused silence with me, and celebrated life's greatest moments with me.

You have given me friends who have advised me, cautioned me, congratulated me, comforted me, encouraged me, and humbled me.

You have given me friends who have shown unconditional love for me, for my family, for other friends, and for their families.

Father, thank You for friends – good friends, loyal friends, godly friends, friends who desire to know You better and challenge me to live like Your Son.

Amazing Things Are Happening Here

The sign outside the New York hospital reads: "Amazing Things Are Happening Here." Truer words were never spoken. Amazing things were happening.

But I am getting a little ahead of myself. For this first-time grandfather, the last nine months have brought many amazing things. It began with a question from our son and daughter-in-law: Are you ready to be grandparents? As the news spread to friends and family other questions followed.

QUESTION: Will you go New York when the baby is born?

ANSWER: Absolutely!

QUESTION: Do they know whether it is a boy or a girl?

ANSWER: They know it is a baby.

QUESTION: Do they have names?

ANSWER: They do but they are not telling.

QUESTION: What do you want to be called?

ANSWER: I really don't care as long as I'm called. Maybe Papa.

QUESTION: Are you excited?

ANSWER: Are you kidding me? How can I not be excited? My son and his wife are having a baby. Yes, I am excited! Out of my head excited!

Then something amazing happened.

You see, I spotted the sign as we stood outside the hospital waiting for a taxi to take us back to the apartment after having spent the day waiting for the arrival of our granddaughter. Amazing things were happening.

For nine months, they were the mother-to-be and the dad-to-be. For nine months, schedules were altered to accommodate the sickness and the discomfort. Plans were altered. More rest was needed. More care was taken. Normal activities were no longer normal. There were days of extreme excitement, and there were days of intense anxiety about the future. Then something amazing happened.

Nine months is a long time to wait and wonder, to anticipate and speculate, to wish and to pray, and to answer questions. Is it a boy or a girl? Do you know? Do you want to know? How big is he or she? Which do you hope it is? How much weight have you gained? What is your due date? Have you picked out a name? What is the name? Who is your doctor? How are you feeling? Oh, don't forget: What do you think about this, Daddy? Nine months of hoping for good health and a safe delivery. Then something amazing happened.

As the due date came and passed, more adjustments were made. More questions were asked. More waiting. A new date was set. The anxiety grew. The days got longer. The waiting continued. Then something amazing happened.

The message was sent: "Heading to the hospital soon." Flights were cancelled. New flights were booked. Amazing things happened.

After months of waiting, it came down to hours of waiting and wondering and hoping and praying. "Lord, please let us get there in time." "Lord, please keep them safe." "Lord, please take care of them." Then something amazing happened.

For several hours, the mother labored as the daddy comforted and reassured. The pain grew more intense (so I'm told). Minutes turned into hours. Then an amazing thing happened. Isabel Taylor was born. She made her appearance. She was safe. Mom was safe. Dad was thrilled. She is healthy. She is beautiful. She is perfect. She is amazing. Amazing things were happening.

When I saw my daughter-in-law's face as she held her daughter and lovingly looked at her baby I saw no signs of frustration because of the months of carrying the baby. I saw no regret over the pain she had just gone through. I saw peace. I saw complete contentment. Something amazing happened here.

When I saw my son, I saw joy in his eyes, I heard the excitement in his voice, and I felt his delight that he had done exactly what he needed to do and that he was exactly where God wanted him to be. I saw no fatigue. I saw sheer peace and contentment. Something amazing happened here.

When I held my granddaughter for the first time and looked at her through my tear-filled eyes, I saw a miracle of God. I saw beauty. I saw perfection. I saw love. Something amazing happened here.

The Proverb reads, *Children's children are a crown to the aged, and parents are the pride of their children.* (Proverbs 17:6)

The sign outside the New York hospital reads: "Amazing Things Are Happening Here."

You have no idea!

God is amazing! Life is amazing! Being married is amazing! Being a parent is amazing! Being Papa to a beautiful granddaughter…well, we are only beginning to learn just how amazing that is.

What Will They Say?

I sat in the packed church sanctuary for the memorial service of a minister friend who served one church for forty years. Co-workers, friends, and family members shared memories and offered praise for a life well lived. Videos and music illustrated the fullness and richness of this good man's life. There were tears, there was laughter, there was joy, and there was sorrow.

As I listened, I wondered, "What if that were me? What would they say? Would people talk about what a fun guy I was? Would they share stories of how I enjoyed the journey? Would they talk about how much I loved people and how much I loved the Lord? Would they talk about my making a difference in the lives of people? Would my co-workers talk of what a privilege and joy it was to work with me? Would it be a celebration of my life or would it be a sad memorial for a man whose life had simply come to an end?"

I'm not fishing for affirmation or compliments. For me to spend the time during and after a memorial service reflecting on my own life is fairly normal. Maybe a bit more at this service because he was a minister, so close to my own age, and such a good guy.

These reflective thoughts may have been more intense after having had contact with two men earlier in the week who have helped shape my life in very powerful ways. The conversations with these two men reminded me of the commitment I made many years ago to live *life to the full* (John 10:10). All of this together reminded me of who I want to be, who I have tried to be, and the legacy I want to leave. It caused me to recommit myself to throw off distractions that keep me from living the life I want to live and the life I believe the Lord wants me to live.

A few months back I designed a bracelet. You know the bracelets I'm talking about. The colorful rubberized kind that so many wear. After wearing a couple of different ones for several years I decided to combine them into one of my own.

The message of my bracelet is simple and formed out of Scripture:

No Complaints!

Do everything without grumbling or arguing, so that you may become blameless and pure, "children of God without fault in a warped and crooked generation." Then you will shine among them like stars in the sky as you hold firmly to the word of life. – Philippians 2:14-16

No Fear!

For I am the Lord your God who takes hold of your right hand and says to you, Do not fear; I will help you. – Isaiah 41:13

Finish Strong

For I am already being poured out like a drink offering, and the time for my departure is near. I have fought the good fight, I have finished the race, I have kept the faith. Now there is in store for me the crown of righteousness, which the Lord, the righteous Judge, will award to me on that day—and not only to me, but also to all who have longed for his appearing. – 2 Timothy 4:6-8

As a companion to those three phrases, I want people to be able to look at me and remember me as a man who followed Paul's instructions: *Walk by the Spirit.* (Galatians 5:16) To live a life that is characterized by these qualities: *But the fruit of the Spirit is love, joy, peace, forbearance, kindness, goodness, faithfulness, gentleness and self-control. Against such things there is no law. Those who belong to Christ Jesus have crucified the flesh with its passions and desires. Since we live by the Spirit, let us keep in step with the Spirit. Let us not become conceited, provoking and envying each other.* – Galatians 5:22-26

Somewhat like Joshua, you can choose to live however you please to live, but as for me, and I hope my household, I'm going to live like this.

No Fear.

No Complaints.

Finish Strong.

A life characterized by love, joy, peace, patience, kindness, goodness, gentleness, faithfulness, and self-control.

Myrleen

Just saying the name awakens an abundance of memories. Since moving to Brunswick, Georgia, in 1986, Myrleen and Bobby have been names used by my family to describe two people who represented the very essence of love, encouragement, generosity, and respect. Just a little over ten years ago I was honored to conduct Bobby's funeral service, and this week I will do the same for Myrleen.

Myrleen and Bobby were members of the church where I preached. For all those in our little church Myrleen was known for her kindness, her thoughtfulness, and her desire to make sure all things were done with efficiency, excellence, and style. She could have easily been compared to the woman of Acts 9 described as, *always doing good and helping the poor* (Acts 9:36), and the woman in Mark 14 who *did what she could* (14:1-9).

That was Myrleen. She was always doing good and helping someone. She did what she could to help the lady who cleaned her house. She did what she could to help the lady who ironed Bobby's shirts. She did what she could to help the young couple at church. She did what she could to help widows. She did what she could to help anyone she came in contact with who needed help.

She loved her family. Her sons and her daughter and her grandchildren were the lights of her life. When they needed her, she was there. When they needed help, she was ready to help. She could be tough when she needed to be, but there was never a doubt that she loved.

She loved flowers – especially daylilies. She loved having them in the house. She loved having them on the table. She loved seeing them grow around her house. And she loved sharing them with her friends.

She loved, and she was loved. She loved her church family and was loved by her church family. She loved the people with whom she worked and was loved by people with whom she worked. She loved her old friends and was loved by her old friends. She loved her new friends and was loved by her new friends just as much. Part of the reason she loved so much was because she had experienced so much love. Part of the reason she was loved so much is because the people she loved knew the love was genuine and real.

For these many years, God has blessed our family by allowing Myrleen to fill the role of substitute grandmother to our children and a surrogate mother to me.

She knew the Lord loved, and she wanted to please Him more than anything else. Because of her strong work ethic, she sometimes wondered if she had done enough to please Him and to get into Heaven. When she left her frail and weary earthly body early Saturday morning there is no doubt in my mind that the Lord welcomed her into His presence and assured her that she had done what she could to help people in need and that it is now time to enjoy the reward of her labors.

Thank You, Lord, for allowing Myrleen to fill a tremendously important void in my life and for letting me love and be loved by her. Rest well, Myrleen, enjoy the fruit of your good life. You will be missed, and I will never forget that you loved me.

My Big Sister

Eugenia LaVerne Gilbert (July 8, 1943 – October 19, 2015)

Ten years older, she was always there. When a bigger kid on the school bus did what today would be considered bullying, she came to my rescue. When our mother died as a young woman, Genia accepted the role as the matriarch of our family at a very early age. Although physical stature would provide no evidence to prove it, Genia was my big sister.

To her husband for over fifty years, she was his wife. Devoted to him and his family, she stood by him, with him, and at times when it was necessary, she stood for him. She loved him, honored him, served him, and was loved, honored, and served by him. Together they provided assurance that marriages can last, that faithfulness is not old fashioned, and genuine servanthood is possible.

To her two children, she was their mother. She loved them unconditionally, taught them, talked to them, guided them, comforted them, cared for them, showed them how to live and helped them understand what it means to be a parent. They loved her, listened to her, followed her guidance, appreciated her comfort and care, and learned about life from her.

To three, she was their grandmother. She loved them with an everlasting love. She praised them. As she did with her two children, she talked when she need to talk and listened when she needed to listen, prayed constantly, and reminded them often how proud she was of them.

To a seemingly endless number of people, she was their Bible teacher. Through Sunday School classes, private conversations, cards, letters, emails, and even texts, she shared the Word and messages of hope and encouragement. Along with being a Bible teacher, she was a faithful and passionate prayer warrior. It would be interesting to know how many times in her seventy-two years she promised someone, "Well, I will be praying for you." When she promised it, she would do it.

To some she was a writer. She published a few articles and poems and

I suspect wrote much more that none of us have ever read. She did not make a big deal out of it, and she preferred that others not make a big deal about it either. Not surprising!

To those who worked with her, she was known as a hard worker, a reliable worker, and a trusted employee. If she said she would do it, she did it or explained why she could not. If she accepted the job, the work got done.

To more people than can be counted, she was known as friend. She had life-long friends. Not just acquaintances! New friends became real friends. She was genuine. She was authentic. She was open. She was honest. She was real. She was spiritual. She was fun.

To some, she was a cousin, or a niece, or a sister-in-law, or a mother-in-law, or a neighbor, or a church member. The list of descriptive words that could be attached to all those titles would include all those already used plus devoted, intelligent, responsible, and caring. She was known for her deep and passionate love for the people she called family.

To my own children, and the children of my two brothers, she was a substitute grandmother. We celebrated many Christmases in her home. When my two children were born, she was the first person I called. When she could, she attended their graduations and weddings. Most of us celebrated very few birthdays without receiving a card from her. At Christmas time, she would ship us a package containing her sweet treat specialties: fudge, peanut butter fudge, and divinity. Sometimes I shared it with my children, and a few special friends.

Genia was all these things to all these people. Genia was known for her laughter, for her generosity, for her kindness, for her wisdom, for her faith and her faithfulness, for her loving nature, and for her passion to know God. As I grew up I watched her as she matured as a wife and mother, then a grandmother. I listened as she talked about our parents and grandparents and aunts and uncles and cousins and neighbors and friends of our family. I was the recipient of her prayers and encouraging words.

In some ways, I suppose some would say she stepped in as a substitute mother for me during my teenage years, but mostly she was my big sister. My big sister who has always been there. My big sister who has always assured me that I am loved. My big sister who I could call, or write, or text, or email anytime I needed to share whatever was in my heart. My big sister who often, more often than seems possible, understood my frustrations with life and people and church because she shared those same frustrations with life and people and church.

Genia was many things to many people, but she was my big sister. In the quiet of the funeral home chapel I stood by her casket shortly before her memorial service and told her, "I know you are now in a much better place, and I am glad for you, but I sure am going to miss you." I do. And I will. She was my big sister.

Acknowledgements

These are some of the people I want to acknowledge who have, in one way or another, encouraged me to write in the beginning and then encouraged me to keep writing.

Thank you to C. Bruce White and Maye Weathers from the 7th Street Church of Christ who said, "You need to write a weekly bulletin article. Just call it Norvell's Notes." That's where it all started.

Thank you to those friends and family on that initial mailing list for reading and sharing the Scripture-based, Jesus-centered, life-application thoughts with friends who in turn shared them with some of their friends.

Thank you to a special friend and sister, Debbie King, who has told me many times, "You need to publish these!" Finally! It is done!

Thank you to Brent High and David Matthew at Faithsite.com (Jabez Networks) and to Phil Ware at Heartlight.org, who have shared many of my articles on their websites and made it possible during this twenty-year process for some of these Notes travel all over the world.

Thank you to all the church secretaries and church bulletin editors who have shared my articles with your people (some of you even contacted me and asked for permission).

Thank you for all the readers on Facebook, Twitter, LinkedIn, at Wordpress.com (and possibly others) who have read, "liked," commented, and shared these articles with your friends and family.

Thank you to Dodd Hartness for helping me with photos, editing, setting up websites, and in many more ways than I can recall. You have helped more than you will ever know…maybe you do know.

Thank you to Natalie Brooke Breazeale, who in the last eighteen months has edited my articles before I send them out to the public.

Thanks to all of you who tolerated (or tried to tolerate) my misspelled words, bad punctuation, missing words, and other grammatical errors before I decided I needed someone to edit my articles.

Thank you to Stephanie Pigg for reconnecting me with Brandon Wagoner and encouraging me with, "You should do this!"

Finally, and especially, I thank Brandon Wagoner and Grassleaf Publishing for inviting me, guiding me, and encouraging me to transform this collection of messages into a volume of published writing known as *Until Hope Returns*. It has been an exciting journey and glad we have gone through it together.

Many thanks to Anne Donnell for her remarkable editing work.

About the Author

Tom, the youngest of four children, grew up in Hope, Arkansas, in a family with deep spiritual roots that have helped him cultivate a heart for loving God and loving people. His college education began at Arkansas State University where he met his wife Kim.

Tom and Kim have been married for forty-two years and have two children: Grant and Bethany and their two daughters live in Brooklyn, New York (with another child on the way); Laura and Alex and their two daughters live in Buda, Texas. For forty-one years Tom served in various roles of full-time ministry (youth, college, preaching, and family ministry), with churches in Mississippi, Georgia, Virginia, and Tennessee.

In 2016, he retired from preaching full-time, but not from ministry, to write a new chapter of his life where he is focused on life coaching, teaching, and writing. He has been writing and publishing *A Norvell Note* for twenty years.

Tom and Kim live near Austin, Texas, where Tom is embarking on a new mission with a hospice company. His favorite pastimes include spending time with Kim and their children and grandchildren, writing, playing golf, and watching sports.